SAVE

AMERICA,

SAVE!

SAVE AMERICA, SAVE!

THE SECRETS OF A SUCCESSFUL 401(k) PLAN

CHARLES D. EPSTEIN, The 401k Coach®

Advantage.

Published by Advantage, Charleston, South Carolina.
Member of Advantage Media Group.

ADVANTAGE is a registered trademark and the Advantage colophon is a trademark of Advantage Media Group, Inc.

Printed in the United States of America.

ISBN: 978-1-59932-546-0
LCCN: 2014955690

Book design by Megan Elger.

This publication is designed to provide accurate and authoritative information in regard to the subject matter covered. It is sold with the understanding that the publisher is not engaged in rendering legal, accounting, or other professional services. If legal advice or other expert assistance is required, the services of a competent professional person should be sought.

Paychecks for Life®, The Desirement Mortgage® Calculator, and Desirement Planning® are registered trademarks of The 401k Coach® and are being used with the express permission of The 401k Coach, LLC. They may not be used or copied without the express permission of The 401kCoach, LLC.

The views and opinions expressed in *Save America, Save!* are only those of the author and any contributing authors. *Save America, Save!* discusses many strategies and techniques that may not be appropriate for every situation. You should consult with your advisors, including tax and legal, before making any decisions based on the content of this book.

Advantage Media Group is proud to be a part of the Tree Neutral® program. Tree Neutral offsets the number of trees consumed in the production and printing of this book by taking proactive steps such as planting trees in direct proportion to the number of trees used to print books. To learn more about Tree Neutral, please visit **www.treeneutral.com**. To learn more about Advantage's commitment to being a responsible steward of the environment, please visit **www.advantagefamily.com/green**

Advantage Media Group is a publisher of business, self-improvement, and professional development books and online learning. We help entrepreneurs, business leaders, and professionals share their Stories, Passion, and Knowledge to help others Learn & Grow. Do you have a manuscript or book idea that you would like us to consider for publishing? Please visit **advantagefamily.com** or call **1.866.775.1696.**

This book is dedicated to America's entrepreneurs, who risk their capital, personal energy, and ideas every day to create the businesses that employ American workers. Thank you for the jobs you create and the benefits that you provide that make a more prosperous future possible for working America.

Throughout the course of this book there are particular references that the author makes to the financial concept of creating "Paychecks for Life."

The author's reference to Paychecks for Life is not an actual W-2 paycheck that you would receive from an employer. It refers to a concept of creating an income stream from your retirement plan throughout your lifetime after you have stopped working.

There is no guarantee implied by the author that this income will be created if you do invest in your 401(k) plan. The reader should understand that withdrawals from a 401(k) are not a guaranteed amount and there is no guarantee that by saving money in your 401(k) plan you will be assured of a retirement income for life. Withdrawals from a 401(k) plan differ markedly from earning results from a salary or wages (a paycheck) because this type of income is not generated in the same manner and differs in how much income is generated, growth potential, tax treatment and renewability.

The readers should always seek the advice of a knowledgeable financial advisor and or accountant when planning their retirement and matters pertaining to their personal taxes.

ACKNOWLEDGMENTS

There were many people involved in getting *Save America, Save!* from an idea in the deep recesses of my mind to reality.

First, to Susan Austin for her herculean efforts in extracting this idea from within me and guiding me to that "Big Idea - a-ha moment!" What started out as a 90 minute interview concept has quickly grown into a national movement that will impact the lives of millions of America's workers. Thanks to Dean Jackson and his team at "The 90 Minute Book" for helping craft the first phase of this project. If you are ever looking to write a book quickly go to www.90minutebook.com.

To Adam Witty and his amazing team at Advantage Media Group. Your team was right when they said, "Charlie this idea is too big for a small book!" Thanks to everyone for helping me craft this book project and the book marketing concepts; from the many re-writes, edits, and amazing cover design to the final magical version. We had an incredibly tight time line and you all delivered with exceptional professionalism, energy and enthusiasm. If you are looking to write you first book be certain to speak to Adam Witty at the Advantage Media Group www.advantage family.com. They will serve you beyond your expectations!

To my 401k Coach Team for their dedication, support and belief in our mission to create greater satisfaction, success and significance in the lives of 401(k) advisors, and plan participants.

This book has grown out of all of your commitment to The Big Idea Focus Group master mind program, where I was able to incubate my thinking and test out my ideas which have lead to the evolution of our book.

First, to Amanda Walker, our fearless "Project Manager." You have worked tirelessly to help me vet out the many options and decisions necessary to get this book from idea to reality. You continue to manage the details of making *Save America, Save!* a book that hundreds of advisors can use to grow their business faster, easier and bigger and to impact the successful retirement outcomes of millions of 401(k) participants. To Marie Forest, there is no better steward of our 401k Coach advisor members. Everyday you manage to serve their every concern and "mother" their "scraped-knees" to a healing solution that makes them more successful. To Danielle Hall and her remarkable graphic design abilities which make our mission pop with color and creativity.

To all the 401(k) Advisors in our Big Idea Focus Group and Year One Training Programs. Thank you for your honest and constructive feedback. Your comments have helped make this book more informative for our readers. I believe it will encourage Plan Sponsors to embrace Courageous Plan Design features that will increase their employees chances of creating "Paychecks for Life."

To the team at Epstein Financial Services: Krista Krupa, Leo Polverini, Brian Caine, Lisa Thompson, Sheila Craven and Lorie Epstein. Everyday you live and breathe and deliver all of the concepts and principles we talk about in *Save America, Save!* to our 401(k) Plan Sponsors and Plan Participants. You are amazingly committed to helping our clients create Paychecks for Life and a life with financial independence and dignity. Each and everyone of you make it possible for me to invest the time and energy in writing, and coaching hundreds of advisors across the country to spread our message to "Save America, Save!"

Thank you all. I am forever grateful.

TABLE OF CONTENTS

The MARS Question

I magine that you are at Logan International Airport in Boston, ready for a trip to Los Angeles. You are about to board the plane, when the gate agent comes on the PA system and says, "Ladies and gentlemen, the FAA and the pilot have asked me to make the following announcement. They've asked me to tell you that there is an 85 percent chance that this plane will not make it to the final destination on time and safely. Have a nice flight."

Will you be getting on that plane?

I ask that question of employers who sponsor a 401(k) plan. What I am asking is this: "Why are you boarding your employees onto your company-sponsored 401(k) plan, when there may be the possibility that they won't arrive safely at their final destination?"

I call it the MARS Question. What I am asking is, are you giving your employees the opportunity to make it to retirement with a "Minimum Adequate Rate of Success?" Will they have enough money saved to replace their current income to create Paychecks for Life®?

It's no longer sufficient for you as an employer to simply offer your employees a 401(k) retirement plan. You also need to be focused on how you can assist them to solve their savings crisis.

There are simple incremental steps every plan sponsor of a 401(k) plan can implement to educate, motivate, activate, and engage their employees to save more and invest more. This can take place at both the plan level (what you, the plan sponsor, can do to influence behavioral change in employee savings and investment habits) and at the employee level, with ongoing education.

Now, more than ever, your employees need your assistance and leadership to ensure they will have saved enough money to replace their current income in retirement and can retire with financial independence and reduced financial anxiety.

This book will show how you, as an employer sponsoring a 401(k) retirement plan, can influence and encourage your employees to save enough money to achieve a successful retirement experience.

In this book, I lay out simple strategies that you and your company can implement to help your employees create "Paychecks for Life®" and begin to measure their results on an ongoing basis.

What are the benefits to you as an employer? When your employees feel they are making financial progress, their attitude about themselves and their employer improves. They experience greater gratitude and enthusiasm for their workplace, and their personal performance improves. They will also experience greater confidence that their financial future is bigger than their financial past.

I will share valuable strategies that you and your company can implement to help improve your 401(k) retirement plan and your employees' retirement saving experience. These include:

- Income Replacement Ratio

- Courageous Plan Design

- Auto to the Fifth Power (Auto^5)

- Desirement Planning

- 10-1-Now

- Retirement Metrics of Success

You can begin to implement these strategies immediately with your employees to influence their behavior, impact their retirement success, and improve employee satisfaction—all with little or no additional cost to your company's pocketbook.

This book will show you how to measure and improve your employee's Minimum Adequate Rate of Success so they arrive at their retirement destination "on time and safely."

PART ONE

Our Savings Crisis

WHY AMERICA HAS A SAVINGS CRISIS

One of the big mysteries here in America is why we cannot save more. There is a savings crisis in this country. Countless studies over the past five to ten years show that American workers are not saving enough money to replace their working income so they'll have Paychecks for Life in their retirement years.

The average savings rate in America is stuck somewhere around 5 percent. The average 401(k) account balance, at year end of 2013, was $72,383 and the median account balance was $18,433.[1] At those rates, the majority of Americans will never have enough money saved to retire successfully. They won't have enough money to replace their paychecks. They will either be forced to keep on working or require financial help.

That's why I've written this book. You see, employees, if left to their own devices, just won't be able to save enough without encouragement and support from their employers. I want to show employers how easy it is for them to encourage their employees

1 Employee Benefit Research Institute (ebri.org) Issue Brief, December 2014, No. 408

to save more, by showing them a series of strategies they can implement that will impact employee behavior and simplify the process of saving for a successful retirement.

In addition, *Save America, Save!* is really a call to arms. We need to get America saving more now.

HOW MUCH DO YOU REALLY NEED WHEN YOU RETIRE?

I tell employees, "As a rule of thumb, you need to save at least 10 percent of your pay to replace enough of your current income to have enough money to pay for all the things you're going to desire to do when you retire." If you're in your 20s or 30s, it might be less than 10 percent. If you are over 40, it could be more, between 12–15 percent.

How do you determine how much is enough? In the financial services industry, we use what we call the *income replacement formula* or the *income replacement ratio*. It works like this: On average, you may need to replace 70, 80, 90 percent, or even more of your current income, plus a factor for inflation (depending on your specific situation), so you'll have enough money throughout your retirement years.

Let's look at a simple example: Let's say you're 40 years old, your current income is $50,000, and you want to stop working at age 65. Let's also assume that your house is going to be paid off, and your children are grown and no longer on your "payroll." You probably don't need 100 percent of your current income when you retire, because you don't have all the same expenses. So let's assume you only need to replace 80 percent of your current income at retirement.

Next, we need to take into account the impact that inflation will have on an employee's purchasing power. Fifty years ago, gasoline cost

23 cents a gallon. As I write this, the cost is as high as $4 a gallon, depending on where you live. That's the effect of inflation.

A simple economic definition of inflation is: too much money chasing too few goods. The cost of consumer goods and services keeps going up over time, making your income worth less in purchasing power.

THE RULE OF 72

The Rule of 72 is a great mental math shortcut to estimate the effect of any growth rate. Here's the formula:

72 / (interest rate) = the amount of years your money doubles

This formula is useful for financial estimates and understanding the nature of compound interest. Example: with a consistent 6 percent interest rate on your money, it will take 12 years to double:

$$72 / 6 = 12$$

The Rule of 72 can also help you determine how quickly inflation is eroding your money. Example: If the inflation rate goes from 2 percent to 3 percent, your money will lose half its value 12 years sooner:

$$72 / 2 = 36$$

$$72 / 3 = 24$$

The difference is 12 years.

Let's go back to our example of the 40 year old: His income is $50,000, and let's assume inflation will be 3 percent for the next 25 years. How much money will he need to earn to maintain his current standard of living at age 65?

If we divide 72 by 3 (the annual rate of inflation), we get the number 24, which means in 24 years his $50,000 income will be worth only half, cut to $25,000 in purchasing value. Therefore, 3 percent inflation over 24 years reduces his purchasing power by 50 percent. To put it another way, he will need at least twice as much money to live on, or more than $100,000 a year, by the time he reaches age 65. If he wants to replace 80 percent of that income at retirement, he will actually need at least $80,000 a year to live on and not his current $50,000 salary.

As you can see, inflation really can have an impact on your income replacement ratio. It's vital to factor inflation in when making any projections.

Today, many 401(k) record keepers' websites will calculate an employee's income replacement ratio for them right on their quarterly 401(k) statement. They will convert how much money an employee has saved into a monthly income figure. This is helpful because it begins to get employees to think more in terms of how much their savings will "purchase" in goods and services each month when they retire and how much more they need to save to have enough monthly income to maintain their current standard of living in retirement.

Nonetheless, most workers still don't know what to do to solve the problem of saving enough. They go to work, they earn a living, they pay for everything they have, and nobody is asking them, "How much do you really need to save for a healthy retirement and how can you do it without sacrificing your current lifestyle?"

WHY SOCIAL SECURITY MIGHT NOT BE AVAILABLE FOR YOUR EMPLOYEES

Ask yourself whether you think you will be receiving a Social Security benefit someday. You probably would like to think you will get something, but you might not be all that confident you will.

For the average person working today—and when I say average, I mean making less than $118,500 (which is the maximum Social Security wage base in 2015)—Social Security may only represent 20 percent to 30 percent of the income that person is going to need to live on during their retirement years. That's if there *is* any Social Security when they retire.

Have you looked at your Social Security statement lately? Most people just look at the number on the second page showing how much they can expect at retirement—what their estimated monthly retirement income will be at age 62, 67, or 70. They never take the time to read all four pages of the statement.

The most important part is on page one. Here's what it says:

> "Social Security is a compact between generations. Since 1935, America has kept the promise of security for its workers and their families. Now, however, the Social Security system is facing serious financial problems, and action is needed soon to make sure the system will be sound when today's younger workers are ready for retirement.
>
> "Without changes, in 2033, the Social Security Trust Fund will be able to pay only 77 cents for each dollar of scheduled benefits. We need to resolve these issues soon to make sure Social Security continues to provide a foundation of protection for future generations."

In my opinion, the government is sending a notice saying: "Someday, you could be evicted from this retirement system, because we may not have enough money to pay you these estimated benefits! You may not have Social Security payments to look forward to."

When I lead employee education meetings, I ask them, "How many of you out there think you're going to get Social Security?" Only 20 percent to 30 percent of the workers in the room raise their hand, and it's always the older employees.

No one knows for sure what's going to happen to Social Security. I believe the system will change to an *income means testing program*. In other words, the government will look at how much income you have and, based on a certain income level, not pay any benefits or pay reduced benefits. The government might say that if you receive income over a certain level—let's say $75,000 to $100,000 from all sources, both earned and unearned—you don't really need Social Security and won't receive it.

OPTIMIZING YOUR SOCIAL SECURITY BENEFITS

For many of your employees, Social Security benefits may represent one of their largest financial assets. Unfortunately, most Americans decide when to begin Social Security benefits without any advice. A majority of Americans have no idea how important selecting a Social Security strategy can be. A smart "claiming strategy" can often mean hundreds of thousands of dollars in added benefits over a retiree's lifetime. In 2009, consistent with previous years, 74% of all Social Security claimants started benefits before Full Retirement Age.[2] We offer your employees, a complimentary "Social Security Calculator Report" which will show them how to maximize both their own and their spouse's Social Security benefits.

If you would like to receive a sample Social Security Calculator report, please email us at: info@epsteinfinancial.com and simply request a copy.

WHY A 401(K) IS THE BEST PLACE TO SAVE

It should be clear that it will not be enough for working Americans to rely on Social Security and the government to create a secure retirement. So what do we need to do? How can employers help encourage their employees to save and invest more to be ready for retirement?

The best place to begin is with their employer-sponsored 401(k) plan, because that's where they can save money automatically, through payroll deduction, very easily throughout their working years.

I wrote this book as a handbook for employers who want to impact employee behavior and encourage their employees to create a successful retirement experience for themselves. We like to help employers help their employees create a Paycheck for Life®.

It used to be that employers established a retirement plan for their employees to give them an extra benefit or an incentive, or

2 "Annual Statistical Supplement to the Social Security Bulletin," Social Security Administration, released February 2010.)

to stay competitive. Times have changed. Almost every company offers a 401(k) plan today—and that's why I say they have become America's retirement savings plan.

HOW YOU CAN PERSUADE EMPLOYEES TO BE SMARTER WITH THEIR MONEY

Here's a great thing about the 401(k) plan: The employer can help the employee to save more through automating savings and investing. In this way, they'll save more than they would likely save on simple savings deposits.

I call these automatic features "Auto to the 5th Power" (Auto^5), which I will explain in detail in Part Two. Many advisors to 401(k) plans call this *plan design optimization*. Some in the industry call it *courageous plan design*, because it's meant to influence employee behavior by getting them to increase their savings rates, improve their investment decisions, and solve their income replacement dilemma in a courageous fashion.

If you as an employer implement one or more of these features, you'll receive fiduciary protection from the Pension Protection Act of 2006. The federal government wants to encourage employers to encourage employees to save more. Under the Pension Protection Act of 2006, the government says employers will have fiduciary protection and can't be sued for implementing these features, provided they send out the appropriate and timely communication notices to all the employees and demonstrate they are following a prudent investment process with due diligence for the benefit of their employees and their beneficiaries.

SAVE AMERICA SAVE ACTION STEPS

1. There is a savings crisis in America. Your employees need to save more and you, their employer, can assist them.

2. The income replacement ratio formula is the first step to helping your employees determine how much money they need to save at retirement to create a Paycheck for Life®. Before enrolling your employees into your company sponsored 401(k) plan, be sure to help them calculate this ratio.

3. Social Security was never meant to be a retirement program for working Americans. Your employees need to understand that it may only provide 20-30 percent of their income at retirement. To request a copy of our Social Security Calculator Report simply email us at info@epsteinfinancial.com and say, "Please send me a sample Social Security Calculator report."

4. The 401(k) plan offers a convenient way for your employees to easily save a percentage of their pay each week to help supplement their retirement income.

5. If you sponsor a 401(k) Plan, you can make it much easier for your employees to save enough money to create "Paychecks for Life" by automating the saving and investing process.

PART TWO

THE POWER OF AUTO[5]

TWO TYPES OF INVESTORS

In my experience doing this kind of work, I've discovered there are two types of investors in the world. The first type are the ones who know or think they know how to invest their money. They are self-motivated and have a real interest in managing their own investment choices. The second type are the ones who don't know and do not want to know how to invest their money or what investment options they should choose. They don't have the time, the tenacity, or the education to make informed investment decisions on an ongoing basis.

In my opinion, the majority of employees are in the "don't know, and don't want to know" category.

Here's an even bigger concern: As of June 30th 2014, 401(k) plans held an estimated $4.4 trillion in assets and represented nearly 18 percent of the $24 trillion in U.S. retirement assets. In 2012, about 52 million American workers were active 401(k) participants and there were about 515,000 401(k) plans.[3] Many plans have 30 or more investment options. While many employers...

3 https://www.ici.org/policy/retirement/plan/401k/faqs_401k

may feel choice is a good thing, in the end, they're just confusing the average employee. Left to their own devices, they either choose not to invest because they're confused, or worse, they make the wrong investment decisions based on the wrong investment information.

Employees typically are chasing performance. When they get their 401(k) statements, assuming they even look at them, they fixate on fund performance, which is based on past performance. They use that information as the sole basis for their investment decisions. Invariably, they pick the funds that have had the highest returns—and they do so just when the market turns.

The following chart shows how poorly the average uninformed and uneducated investor has done over the last 20 years. It affirms my belief that America's 401(k) is the largest casino in the country, a crap shoot where employees toss money into a pot and hope for a win, but where, typically, the house wins, and they lose.

THE COST OF UNINFORMED INVESTING

Growth of a hypothetical $100,000 investment
12/31/95 – 12/31/15

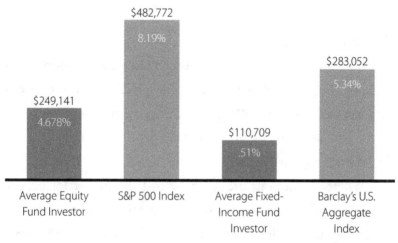

$249,141	$482,772	$110,709	$283,052
4.678%	8.19%	.51%	5.34%
Average Equity Fund Investor	S&P 500 Index	Average Fixed-Income Fund Investor	Barclay's U.S. Aggregate Index

Source: "Quantitative Analysis of Investor Behavior, 2016," DALBAR, Inc. www.dalbar.com

IMPORTANT DISCLOSURES

Data Sources: Investment Company Institute, Standard & Poor's, Barclays Capital Index Products and the Bureau of Labor Statistics

Average stock investor, average fixed income investor, and average asset allocation investor performance results are calculated using data supplied by the Investment Company Institute. Investor returns are represented by the change in total mutual fund assets after excluding sales, redemptions, and exchanges. This method of calculation captures realized and unrealized capital gains, dividends, interest, trading costs, sales charges, fees, expenses, and any other costs. After calculating investor returns in dollar terms, two percentages are calculated for the period examined: Total investor return rate and annualized investor return rate. Total return rate is determined by calculating the investor return dollars as a percentage of the net of the sales, redemptions, and exchanges for each period.

The equity market is represented by the Standard & Poor's 500, an unmanaged index of common stock. The fixed income market is represented by the Barclays Aggregate Bond Index. Inflation is represented by the Consumer Price Index. Indexes do not take into account the fees and expenses associated with investing, and individuals cannot invest directly in any index. Past performance cannot guarantee future results.

TERMINOLOGY & RESEARCH NOTES
AVERAGE INVESTOR

The average investor refers to the universe of all mutual fund investors whose actions and financial results are restated to represent a single investor. This approach allows the entire universe of mutual fund investors to be used as the statistical sample, ensuring ultimate reliability.

[AVERAGE] INVESTOR BEHAVIOR

QAIB quantitatively measures sales, redemptions, and exchanges (provided by the Investment Company Institute) and describes these measures as investor behaviors. The measurement of investor behavior is the net dollar volume of these activities that occur in a single month during the period being analyzed.

[AVERAGE] INVESTOR RETURN (PERFORMANCE)

QAIB calculates investor returns as the change in assets, after excluding sales, redemptions, and exchanges. This method of calculation captures realized and unrealized capital gains, dividends, interest, trading costs, sales charges, fees, expenses, and any other costs. After calculating investor returns in dollar terms (above) two percentages are calculated:

• Total investor return rate for the period
• Annualized investor return rate

Total return rate is determined by calculating the investor return dollars as a percentage of the net of the sales, redemptions, and exchanges for the period.
Annualized return rate is calculated as the uniform rate that can be compounded annually for the period under consideration to produce the investor return dollars.

The average investor - in the "don't know and don't want to know" category - keeps making the wrong bets at the wrong time, just when the table (the market) turns against them. A large percentage of your employees may be in this category. Doesn't it just make sense to help them with the investment decision process?

OVERRIDING EMOTIONS

Emotions can be heated. Emotions can run cool. Emotions can energize you to overcome seemingly impossible challenges, and they can cause you to collapse under intense pressure. Emotions can be an asset or they can be a liability. But one thing is certain: Emotions are always there.

Whether emotions are good or bad depends a lot on the person and the situation, with one exception: where money is concerned. It's a widely held principle among professional investment advisors that emotions provide no benefit when it comes to investing.

Emotions can make you falsely attached to your high-performing funds and tell you to stay away from low-performing funds. They cause false hope. They ignore danger. To put it bluntly, they can cause you to act stupidly.

Let's look at just a few emotions that, if left unchecked, will greatly threaten investment success.

Investing overconfidence

Studies have shown that when people are asked to rate their level of expertise in a variety of areas, including finance, the majority rate themselves above average—a mathematical impossibility. Overconfidence makes investors believe that the success they achieve is due solely to their decisions and that they can do it again. That's a mistaken belief, and one that's difficult for investors to let go of.

Availability bias

Investors can also project their outlooks too far into the future and let that bias their decision making. A classic example of this occurred in December 1996, when Federal Reserve Chairman Alan Greenspan made a speech to the American Enterprise Institute for Public Policy, where he coined the phrase "irrational exuberance" as a warning that stock market prices were inflated according to fundamental valuations.

Few investors listened. They were convinced the market would march higher. After a brief fall, the market continued to climb higher and higher, thus prompting Greenspan to consider that perhaps prices weren't inflated at all.

In September 1998 at the Haas Annual Business Faculty Research Dialogue at the University of California, Greenspan said: "Some of those who advocate a 'new economy' attribute it generally to technological innovations and breakthroughs in globalization that raise productivity and offer new capacity on demand and that have, accordingly, removed pricing power from the world's producers on a more lasting basis."

But the more prophetic words from Greenspan came moments later: "There is one important caveat to the notion that we live in a new economy, and that's human psychology."

People were convinced the market would do nothing but continue to climb. And it did—until 2000 to 2003, when the market shed about 35 percent of its value, leaving investor accounts in shambles. But from 2003 until the end of 2007, the market gained 86 percent[4].

Think of the consequences if you were under-diversified when the market was losing 35 percent, because you firmly believed it

4 S&P 500 Index McGraw Hill Financial 2000-2003 Annual Performance

would continue to grow in the new economy. To make matters worse, what if you sold near the bottom and were afraid to re-enter the market during the subsequent rally? These are very real (and highly likely) situations that occur when investing on emotion.

Loss aversion

Daniel Kahneman and Amos Tversky in their book *Choices, Values, and Frames* showed that people strongly prefer avoiding losses to acquiring gains. In other words, people suffer from risk aversion. The pain felt from a $500 loss is far greater than the satisfaction from a gain of equal size. Therefore, people concentrate their efforts on avoiding losses.

In Kahneman and Tversky's research, a sample of their undergraduates refused to stake $10 on the toss of a coin if they stood to win less than $30. The attractiveness of the gain was not sufficient to compensate for the aversion to the possible loss.

This behavior shouldn't be too surprising, but things got really interesting when the researchers decided to challenge people on their beliefs by adding a related question—with a twist. They asked people if they would prefer an 85 percent chance of losing $1,000 (and, therefore, a 15 percent chance of losing nothing) or a guaranteed loss of $800. A large majority preferred the gamble over the sure loss.

This is risk seeking, because the expectation of the gamble is inferior to the expectation of loss. This shows a critically important point about human psychology and investing: Investors' aversion to loss is so great that it overcomes their aversion to risk. In other words, people despise taking losses so much that they'll overstep their risk boundaries in hopes of avoiding the loss.

That's perhaps the most dangerous of all combined approaches you could take to the financial markets. Unfortunately, it's how we're programmed to behave. In working with your employees, it is essential that both you and they understand this principle of human psychology.

Short of wandering aimlessly through the mountains of Tibet searching for a Buddhist monk, can people completely detach from their emotions? Of course not. So what can they do?

LEVEL-HEADED TECHNOLOGY

Henry Ford used technology to automate the assembly line for cars, and he changed the world in the process. Michael Dell accomplished a similar feat in building computers with just-in-time production.

Likewise, financial professionals have developed computer programs to handle the rote procedures of financial planning and investing. Computer trading or program trading, as it's sometimes called, is just what it sounds like—computer programs are doing the buying and selling.

Large Wall Street firms may, for example, program a computer to sell one million shares of a particular stock if the Dow reaches 10,000, or buy 20,000 shares of IBM if the price falls below its 50-day moving average. Many mutual funds take program trading to a whole new level and allow computers to manage their portfolios by buying or selling shares of particular stocks or indexes as long as certain conditions are met. Profits are taken and losses are limited to specified levels. Rebalancing is automatic. In fact, every single financial decision is automated.

Some financial firms create proprietary computerized systems that individual investors and institutions can access for a fee. These are often called *black box systems* because they're analogous to an unknown box of rules that makes decisions for you. While these systems often outperform the market, they're expensive and charge access fees of 20 percent or more of your profits.

Computers are an excellent tool for investment because they do things automatically (once instructed) and don't have emotions. For those in the business of financial decisions, there's no room for the kind of emotions we've already discussed.

Automating that process through technology is simpler, wiser, and in the end, prudent for both the employee and the fiduciaries.

Let's look at the ways to automate investment decisions to help avoid making costly errors, and to override your employees' emotions.

THE FIVE AUTOMATIC FEATURES (AUTO⁵)

Courageous Plan Design is the first step an employer can take to make an enormous impact on their employees' savings and investment behavior.

There are five features of the Courageous Plan Design:

1. Automatic Enrollment

2. Automatic QDIA

3. Automatic Escalation

4. Automatic Re-enrollment

5. The Stretch Match

Employers should evaluate all five automatic features and then decide which ones they are comfortable implementing.

Before I discuss each one, I want to point out that since these automatic features were introduced in 2006, many employers, especially those with fewer than 100 employees, still have not felt comfortable using one or more of them.

Some employers do not want to upset their employees, and some of them feel paternalistic when enacting these features. They may think that automatically deducting money from an employee's paycheck will upset that employee. I want to say this right up front, especially for the people reading this book who are running retirement plans—the HR directors, CFOs, Presidents and CEOs: What will be upsetting to your employees is *not* using these automated features.

If you do not take action to assist your employees in saving more money or investing appropriately, they'll be more upset when they discover one day that they haven't saved enough for retirement. The worst time for employees to figure that out is when it's too late, when they're already close to retirement. It is imperative that employers make it easy for employees to save and make wiser investment decisions.

I have added a Resource section at the end of the book where you can look up a variety of studies and white papers from various sources that describe the positive benefits of the Auto^5 features.

One of these resources is the website www.retirement madesimpler.org. The site was created by three organizations with three distinct missions: AARP, FINRA (Financial Industry Regulatory Authority), and RSP (the Retirement Security Project).

These three organizations have pooled their varied strengths to help employers and their employees save more effectively.

The website states, "We know that automatic 401(k)s work. Participation rates typically soar to between 85 percent and 95 with these types of plans." The site even offers employers a 401(k) Automatic Toolkit and success stories of other large companies that have implemented these with great success.

Now, let's take a close look at each of those five features of the Courageous Plan Design.

Automatic enrollment

The first is automatic enrollment. This one is easy, and every employer should use it. Here is how it works:

Normally, if you want to get a new employee to enroll in the 401(k) plan, you would ask the employee to fill out an enrollment form and return it in a certain period of time. This can be time consuming for the employer, and ineffective in getting the employee to participate. It ends up being an inefficient process for both the employer and the employee.

A better solution is to simply automate the enrollment process. When an employee becomes eligible to participate in the plan, she receives a letter notifying her that she will be automatically enrolled within 30 days of her start date. Unless the employee notifies the employer that she does not want to participate, the enrollment is automatic, at a minimum percentage of pay.

I believe it's best to enroll employees at the company matching contribution level. If, for example, a company has a matching contribution of 50 percent up to 6 percent, they should automatically enroll their employees at the 6 percent level so that they receive the full matching contribution.

In addition, if an employee who is automatically enrolled does not choose an investment option, then he or she would also be automatically enrolled in the company's "Qualified Default Investment Account" (QDIA) option. (More on this investment option on the following pages.)

Not all employers, however, do these things. Larger companies do—those with 1,000, 10,000, 100,000, or more employees. It's easier on their Human Resource departments. However, 97% of

America's employers have fewer than 100 employees[5], and they don't take advantage of this option. As result, fewer employees enroll in the plans, and we don't get people saving money automatically.

Companies such as McDonald's that have lower-paid hourly workers started using these automatic enrollment features, in 1984, before the Pension Protection Act provided fiduciary protection. The following is taking from a McDonalds case study[6]: All levels of employees hourly and salary were automatically enrolled at 3 percent. McDonalds added a Safe Harbor match in 2002 and eliminated Auto-Enrollment for everyone and participation started dropping for hourly employees. Auto-Enrollment was added back in 2005. Participation remains high at 98.6% by 2010.

If you start deducting money out of an employee's paycheck, and they don't want that to happen, they have the option of opting out. But you can get them in the plan and start them with a good savings habit. It's like exercise. Don't worry about how the employee may feel. Small employers unfortunately tend to worry about the reaction their employees will have if they're automatically enrolled. They tell me, "I don't want to upset my employees." I say, "If they don't have enough money for retirement, they'll be even more upset."

Automatic QDIA

If employees do not make an investment election when being automatically enrolled, they would automatically be invested in the company's Qualified Default Investment Account.

The Department of Labor (DOL) defines a QDIA as an investment fund or model portfolio that's designed to provide

5 Statistics of US Business, total number of entrepreneurs by size and employment, 2012, www.susb.com
6 www.dol.gov/ebsa/pdf/McDonalds062810.pdf

both long-term appreciation and capital preservation through a mix of equity and fixed income exposures. Management of the portfolio's investments must be based on an employee's age of their target retirement date. Investment funds or products lacking either a fixed income or an equity exposure, such as a money market account, will not qualify for QDIA status.

There are a variety of investments that can qualify as your 401(k) plan's QDIA. Balanced funds, which have a mix of equity and bond exposure, typically evenly balanced; lifestyle or lifecycle funds, which will have a mix of equity and bond exposure allocated for conservative, moderate and aggressive investors; and target date funds, which will have a "target retirement date" and adjust its exposure to equity and fixed income gradually getting more conservative the closer an investor is to their retirement. The plan fiduciaries would be required to monitor the QDIAs, on a regular basis, with investment due diligence reviews, to ensure they are a prudent investment choice for their employees.

For the majority of employees today who don't have enough knowledge about how to construct a diversified investment portfolio, it's a better long-term choice to invest in a lifestyle fund, target-based fund, or balanced fund that's well managed and monitored.

Automatic escalation

I believe that automatic escalation is probably the most important auto feature—and here's why. Remember, I stated that Americans need to save at least 10 percent of their pay throughout their working career, if they're ever going to hope to get to their retirement date with an adequate amount of money saved?

If the company only automatically enrolls an employee at 3 percent, or my example of up to the matching 6 percent, we're still a long way off from that required 10 percent savings rate. In addition, if you tell employees they need to save 10 percent right out of the gate, I can tell you from working with thousands of employees in 401(k) plans that they will say, "What, are you crazy? Ten percent? Not going to happen. I have credit card bills to pay. I have my kid's tuition. I'm buying that boat."

A better solution for employees is for them to incrementally increase their savings rate. I have this mantra. It's called "10-1-NOW."

The "10" stands for that 10 percent savings rate, which I tell employees is what they need to save. When an employee says to me, "I can't do that much," I say, "Okay, how much can you save?" If they say 5 percent, I say, "Great. Start with that amount and then increase it by just 1 percent a year until you get to 10 percent." Most employees say, "Okay, I can do that; one percent, no problem."

And then they don't do it. It's human nature. They forget. They don't remember to increase it a year later. That's why, as an employer, you need to automate the decision process for them, NOW! The "now" stands for "do it *now*." Automate that additional 1 percent savings rate a year. The employee just needs to tell the employer, "I want you to increase my percentage every year by 1 percent or even 2 percent, until I get to 10 percent." The problem is most employees won't even remember to tell the employer.

Automatic escalation solves that problem. Each year, the employer automatically sends out a notice to every employee that their contribution will be automatically increased by 1 percent. That way, they don't forget to do it.

To drive home the power of this, take a look at the following chart. I call it the 10-1-NOW Mantra chart.

10-1-NOW

Base Salary: $40,000 **Average Rate of Return: 6.00%** **Average Salary Increase: 0.00%**

Year	10% per year Susan			5% Now + 1%/yr until 10% George			5% forever Morgan		
	Annual Savings	Earnings	Balance	Annual Savings	Earnings	Balance	Annual Savings	Earnings	Balance
1	$4,000	$0	$4,000	$2,000	$0	$2,000	$2,000	$0	$2,000
5	$4,000	$1,050	$22,548	$3,600	$675	$15,521	$2,000	$525	$11,274
10	$4,000	$2,758	$52,723	$4,000	$2,226	$43,320	$2,000	$1,379	$26,362
15	$4,000	$5,044	$93,104	$4,000	$4,331	$80,520	$2,000	$2,522	$46,552
20	$4,000	$8,102	$147,142	$4,000	$7,149	$130,302	$2,000	$4,051	$73,571
25	$4,000	$12,196	$219,458	$4,000	$10,920	$196,922	$2,000	$6,098	$109,729
30	$4,000	$17,674	$316,233	$4,000	$15,966	$286,074	$2,000	$8,837	$158,116
35	$4,000	$25,004	$445,739	$4,000	$22,720	$405,380	$2,000	$12,502	$222,870
40	$4,000	$34,814	$619,048	$4,000	$31,757	$565,039	$2,000	$17,407	$309,524
45	$4,000	$47,942	$850,974	$4,000	$43,851	$778,697	$2,000	$23,971	$425,487
50	$4,000	$65,510	$1,161,344	$4,000	$60,035	$1,064,621	$2,000	$32,755	$580,672

This is a hypothetical example and not representative of any specific product.

It's an example of three employees, Susan, George, and Morgan. They all make the same amount of money, $40,000 a year. They are all 30 years old, and we are going to assume they can all make an average of 6 percent on the savings each and every year. Susan says, "No problem. I can save 10 percent of my pay every year." She saves the 10 percent religiously every year and by the time she's 65, assuming her money grows at 6 percent, she has $445,739. Pretty good.

George, however, says he can't save 10 percent. "I've got too many expenses," he says. "I can only save 5 percent." George agrees to increase his contribution by 1 percent each year until he gets to 10 percent. He does it automatically. In 35 years, he has $405,380. He's only about $40,000 dollars less than Susan's total. Not bad.

Meanwhile, Morgan also promises to start at 5 percent and increase by 1 percent each year. Then guess what she doesn't do? She doesn't increase it by 1 percent per year. And when she's at retirement in 35 years, she only has $222,870.

It's amazing, isn't it? By NOT increasing her contribution by just that 1 percent a year, she has $200,000 dollars LESS than Susan. I call that "the $200,000 mistake!"

That's why we want employers to institute automatic escalation, because they're really doing the employees a disservice when they don't. When employees see the 10-1-Now chart, its impact is remarkable. Employees see this $200,000 mistake and say, "I don't want to be like Morgan. Sign me up for automatic escalation right now!" It is not uncommon for us to see employees even increase their savings rate by 3–4 percent overall.

For our readers, if you would like a FREE copy of the 10-1-Now Mantra Chart to hand out to your employees, e-mail us at info@epsteinfinancial.com and simply say, "Please send me a copy of the 10-1-Now Mantra Chart."

Again, employees can opt out of that automatic increase. With every one of these automatic features, an employee just has to notify the employer and say, "Don't automatically enroll me in the plan. Don't automatically put me in that Qualified Default Investment Account. Don't automatically increase my contribution every year." An employee is always in control.

Automatic re-enrollment

Remember when I said that a large percentage of employees do not have the wisdom or experience to make proper investment decisions? They just don't have enough information to make the best choices for themselves, or to know when to adjust their investment allocation over long periods of time as their tolerance for risk changes and they get closer to retirement.

A multitude of other factors go into making good investment choices: building a well-diversified portfolio, managing investment fees and expenses, rebalancing investments on a regular basis, and again, adjusting investment allocation as one gets closer to retirement to avoid taking too much or too little risk. More often than not, most employees would be better served if they had just invested in a managed account—either that lifestyle fund, target-date fund, or even a balanced fund.

Here's what automatic re-enrollment is: Once a year, the employer sends out a notification letter telling every employee in the plan, "We're going to have an open enrollment period within the next 30 days of the receipt of this letter." If an employee does not respond to the employer, "Do not change my current investment allocations," then 100 percent of their 401(k) balance will be transferred into the QDIA—in this case, the target-date fund, based on their age.

Studies show that when this is done, about 60 percent[7] of participants default into QDIA funds, and they are much better off. Again, if employees do not want their investment choices changed, all they need to do is notify the employer, "Don't move my money."

As a plan trustee fiduciary, you're going to receive fiduciary protection for all these automatic features, including the automatic re-enrollment process. Many employers tell me they are concerned about this feature because they are moving an employee's money out of what he or she had originally selected into one of these funds.

I remind those employers that they will have fiduciary protection under the Pension Protection Act of 2006, provided that: (1) they are giving the appropriate notice, in a timely fashion; (2) employees have the ability to opt out; (3) the target-date fund is the plan's QDIA; and (4) the plan sponsor trustees are performing ongoing prudent investment due diligence reviews on the target-date fund (QDIA) and documenting their process.

The Stretch Match

This really gets to human psychology and behavioral finance by "incentivizing" employees to save a greater percentage of their pay.

---

7 Using Re-enrollment to Improve Participant Investing and Provide Fiduciary Protections, a white paper by Fred Reish & Bruce Ashton, Drinkle Biddle & Reath LLP, March 2014

As an employer, you can influence employee savings rates simply by adjusting your company's current matching formula.

If the long-term goal is to get employees to save a greater percentage of their pay (10%), a better way to do this is to match a smaller percentage of their pay up to a higher company-matched percentage.

For example, let's say you're currently matching 50 percent on the dollar up to the first 6 percent of an employee's savings. You actually are building in a disincentive for your employees to save more than 6 percent of their pay. If the goal is to get your employees to be saving 10 percent of their pay, this type of match is not sufficient to get the job done.

Where's the incentive? Why would an employee save more than 6 percent if the company isn't going to match beyond 6 percent? Employees tell me all the time, "I'm only going to save 6 percent of my pay, because that's all my employer will match." Who does that hurt most? It doesn't really hurt the employer. It harms the employees, who need to save 10 percent or more but don't because they feel, "What's the point, since I don't get any more than a 6% match from my employer?"

This type of company match is really a negative influence. What we want is a matching formula that's a positive influence on employee behavior.

Let's look at a better matching formula. One that gets both the employer and the employee to "stretch" their contributions and achieve a better result. In the process we can use a "positive" financial incentive to influence employees' savings behavior. The following chart shows how to use Behavioral finance to you and your employees advantage. The current matching 401(k) formula is 50% on the first 6% of an employees pay. This type of match costs the employer 3% of payroll for every employee that contributes to the plan. However, as we have already discussed, it does not incentivize employees to save 10% of their pay—only 6%. If instead, this employer was to change their matching contributions to 50% on the first 2% and 25% on the next 8% of pay, employees would have (and want) to save 10% of their pay to get 100% of the employers matching contribution.

STRETCH MATCH DESIGN

Salary Deferral	Current Sample	Stretch Match Sample
10%	-	25%
9%	-	25%
8%	-	25%
7%	-	25%
6%	50%	25%
5%	50%	25%
4%	50%	25%
3%	50%	25%
2%	50%	50%
1%	50%	50%
Matching Formula	50% up to 6%	50% on first 2% 25% on next 8%

Some employers may say, "I don't want to spend any more money than in my current matching formula." But that's not the case: The out-of-pocket cost is the same as the original 50 percent on the first 6 percent match. It still comes out to a 3 percent employer maximum out-of-pocket expense.

However, for the employees who want to get that full match, that full 3 percent of company money, now they have to save 10 percent instead of 6 percent to get it. We have positively influenced employees' behavior to save more by stretching to achieve that 10 percent targeted savings rate. At no additional cost to you, you have incentivized your employees to save 4 percent more!

THE SAFE HARBOR MATCH

A plan sponsor may elect to contribute Safe Harbor minimum contributions to a 401(k) plan and thereby avoid Actual Deferral Percentage (ADP) testing of pre-tax elective deferrals and after-tax Roth elective deferral contributions (elective deferrals) and/ or Actual Contribution Percentage (ACP) testing of employer matching contributions.

There are three safe harbor matching formulas that satisfy the ADP test.

1. Safe harbor non-elective contribution. The employer may make a non-elective contribution equal to at least 3% of compensation to all eligible non-highly compensated (NHCE) and highly compensated (HCE) employees.

2. Safe Harbor (BASIC) matching contribution. Alternatively, the employer may match; (a) 100% of the employee salary deferral up to 3% of compensation, AND (b) match 50% of the employee salary deferral from 3% to 5% compensation.

3. Safe harbor alternative (ENHANCED) matching contribution. The employer may make a different rate of matching contribution to satisfy the matching contribution safe harbor if the following are met:

   □ The contribuiton is a fixed matching contribution;

- The rate of any matching contribution in the plan does not increase as an employee's rate of elective deferral increases;

- The safe harbor matching contribution amount for each employee in the aggregate is at least equal to the amount that would have been contributed under the safe harbor matching formula described in Safe Harbor (BASIC) matching contribution (#2). An example of this type of safe harbor would be a 100% match on the first 4% of an employee contribution.

I mention these "safe harbor" contribution designs, because, if you, as an employer, currently use a safe harbor match design and you switch to the "stretch-match" design, you will most likely be giving up your safe harbor and your plan will be subject to ADP and/or ACP testing. This, along with the timing of when you make a change in your current matching formula, will effect your ultimate decision in amending or changing your current company matching formula to a "stretch match" plan design.

A WORD OF CAUTION

Automatic 401(k) investing provides enormous benefit to employees. As with any benefit, though, there can be drawbacks, and it's important to be aware of the potential pitfalls.

The major drawback to any automated process is that it can lure investors into a false sense of confidence. Automation can make them complacent. They may feel there's no need to participate in the process because it all appears to be taken care of.

As nice as a fully automated investment process would be, these features require involvement in various parts of the process. Autopilot does not replace the pilot. Cruise control does not replace the driver. Instead, these features make some parts of the flying and driving easier. They're not intended to take over completely.

That's also true for the automatic features available for plan investing. There are decisions to make and goals to set.

How much money does the employee need for retirement? How much must be contributed to reach those goals? What risks is the employee willing to take and wanting to avoid?

Automatic 401(k) features cannot answer these and other important questions. Without answers, the employee will be unable to navigate safely, just as you can't go to sleep in the back seat of your car because you're using cruise control. Don't think for a moment that these automatic features do everything.

Planning requires an active role. These processes won't automatically bring success to your employees, but they'll make some of the most important decisions easier and more consistent. They'll also limit the negative impact of emotions—this could go a long way in helping your employees create Paychecks for Life.

SAVE AMERICA SAVE ACTION STEPS

1. There are two types of investors: those who know how to save and invest for a secure retirement and those who don't want to know.

2. Take advantage of Auto[5]:

   □ Automatic enrollment

   □ Automatic QDIA

   □ Automatic increase

   □ Automatic re-enrollment

   □ The Stretch Match

3. As an employer, you must demonstrate leadership and establish a courageous plan design that will automatically get your employees into the 401(k) plan and saving an increasing amount of their paychecks (1-2 percent per year). Studies show that when automatic features are used, 70-90 percent[8] of employees opt in to the 401(k) plan, stay in the plan, and allow their contributions to be automatically increased each year.

4. The 10-1-Now Mantra is a great communication piece to get your employees to enthusiastically increase their contribution by 1 percent each year. Request a copy at info@epsteinfinancial.com.

8 www.retirementmadesimpler.org. 401k success stories and automatic 401(k) directory.

5. Use the Stretch Match Plan Design formula to influence your employees' saving behavior. You can "stretch" your matching contribution, without increasing your budget, and help your employees reach a 10 percent savings rate.

6. Remember, the Pension Protection Act of 2006 offers you fiduciary protection when you use Auto[5].

PART THREE

YOUR ROLE AS A FIDUCIARY

B efore we take a closer look at how to educate and encourage your workforce to save more, let's look at what an employer should be doing as a plan fiduciary to ensure employees receive a good selection of investment options at a reasonable price.

If you're an employer and you sponsor a 401(k) plan, you have a fiduciary responsibility to do what's in the best interest of your employees. Employers must remember that a 401(k) plan is established under ERISA (the Employee Retirement Income Security Act of 1974) for the exclusive purpose of providing benefits to participants and their beneficiaries.

As a plan fiduciary, you have a *duty of loyalty* and a *duty of prudence*. You must be loyal to your participants and their beneficiaries, and avoid any conflicts of interest or prohibited transactions. You must act prudently in managing the plan and the plan's investments. That means you must have a repeatable process to monitor the plan's investments, and hire and fire managers if they are not performing to certain metrics.

You must make sure the services provided by your record keeper, your third-party administrator, your plan advisor, and your auditor are necessary for the management of the plan and that the fees they charge are reasonable. You can determine whether they are reasonable by benchmarking the plan fees on a regular basis.

Fee Benchmarking and RFP

ERISA, encourages plan sponsors to do a full vendor benchmarking comparison of all their vendors every 3-5 years. This type of analysis should benchmark the plan fees, funds, and services to at least 4 competing record-keeping providers.

If you are an owner of a company or the CFO or head of Human Resources, you want to focus your time and energy on managing the success of your company and not the plan. You can hire what are called prudent expert service providers to help meet your roles and responsibilities as a plan fiduciary. This is a way to outsource responsibility for managing the day-to-day operations of the plan. These fiduciary service providers can be:

1. A 3(21) limited scope fiduciary;

2. A 3(38) discretionary fiduciary; and

3. A 3(16) plan administrator.

INVESTMENT CHOICES SHOULD BE LIMITED

Because of the two types of investors in a company's 401(k) plan—those who know and those who don't know how to invest—it is critical that an employer offer a diversified and robust investment lineup.

It may also make sense to limit the number of investment choices down to 16–18 funds. Any more, and you may just end up confusing most employees.

Professor Barry Schwartz, in his book *The Paradox of Choice*, calls this "choice overload." There are many behavioral studies that prove that fewer choices actually encourage people to take action. In the end, that's what we want: more employees to take action and participate in the plan.

Plan fiduciaries should consider that their 401(k) has a well-diversified investment fund lineup. You should consider having an investment option in each major asset class. You should also consider offering a low-cost index fund in every major investment category, including large-cap, mid-cap, small-cap, international, and bonds.

In addition, it should have that one QDIA that we talked about, either a lifestyle, target-date, or balanced fund. That actually would mean six to eight funds, because it would have a conservative fund all the way up to a very aggressive fund at different "target-date" ages. The majority of employees will be better off in those lifestyle or target-date funds.

Employers may wish to offer a managed account that provides more specific individualized investment guidance for employees and for those willing to pay an extra management fee for this advice. All investment options need to be monitored on a regular basis, with a system for changing managers who underperform based on specific investment criteria.

All of this will be enormously helpful in ensuring that employees have adequate options to achieve their short-term and long-term retirement goals, provided they take a balanced approach to their investments.

SMART WAYS FOR EMPLOYEES TO DIVERSIFY

Once your employees contribute money to a 401(k), the question is where should they invest it.

The first rule of successful investing is to diversify among a broad range of asset classes that behave differently and are in different markets.

Mutual funds are a great investment choice for employees, for a variety of reasons. First, a single investment, no matter how small, in one mutual fund allows them to gain control of many stocks or bonds quickly and efficiently. Second, unlike with individual stocks, mutual funds allow people to buy a fractional share (less than one share), which means your employees can always invest 100 percent of their money, regardless of the fund price.

Mutual funds can be divided into two camps: actively managed funds and passively managed index funds (exchange traded funds, or ETFs, are classified as passively managed index funds).

An **actively managed fund** is one in which the fund manager has discretion over the selection of investments (e.g., stocks, bonds, cash, etc.) and how long investments are held.

Passively managed index funds, or ETFs, typically mimic a specific stock or bond market index, which is why they're referred to as index funds. An index fund manager is constrained to holding the same stocks or bonds as the index that he or she is attempting to emulate. Passively managed index funds and ETFs tend to have lower expenses and turnover than do actively managed funds.

One useful function of a professional investment advisor is educating employees on an appropriate asset allocation consistent with each employees' specific investment needs, circumstances, and preferences in mind. An employee can choose to use actively managed funds, passively managed index funds, or a combination of the two, depending on which options you provide in the 401(k) plan.

Asset classes

For diversification to work, it's essential that your employees' portfolios represent a wide range of investment asset classes. Each mutual fund they hold must complement the others. The funds should behave differently, be in different markets, and work over different time periods.

As part of a prudent investment due diligence process, you should consider offering individual funds in the following investment categories:

- US stock funds
- Large-cap
- Mid-cap
- Small-cap
- Non-US stock funds
- Developed companies
- Emerging markets
- Real estate
- Resource funds
- Natural resources
- Commodities
- US bond funds
- Aggregate bonds

- Inflation-protected bonds

- Non-US bond funds

- International bonds

- Cash

Risk reduction

Greater diversification is key to managing investment risk. Risk can be measured in different ways:

Volatility of return in a portfolio: The typical measure of volatility in an investment portfolio is standard deviation of return, a statistical measure that's often reported alongside the mean (or average) annualized return of an investment. A mutual fund with a high standard deviation of return would be considered a high-risk fund.

Cumulative return: Cumulative return is a measure of how much an investor's actual account balance increased or decreased over a specific period of time.

Frequency of portfolio loss: This definition of risk measures how often an investment account has lost money over a specified time. *Underwater* is a term used to describe an account that has a lower current balance than the starting balance. The biggest mistake most investors make is to look for the highest-performing funds. They feel that selecting lower-performing funds only creates a drag on overall performance. This is not necessarily true. We don't know for sure what's going to happen in the business world.

Naïve diversification

Helping your employees to understand the idea behind diversification and the power it offers is not enough—they must make sure they are diversifying correctly. As with any technique, there's a right way and a wrong way.

New investors often attempt to diversify by choosing many high-performing funds; that's not true diversification. Purchasing many separate yet highly related funds is a technique that academics call *naïve diversification*. It's an inexperienced attempt to manage risk. While it's better than putting all of your money into a single fund, it reduces risk only slightly.

The proper way to diversify is to put dollars in diverse asset classes. Portfolios need some "risk" classes and some "safe" classes. An employee may, for example, choose high-growth stock funds, emerging market funds, and bond funds. Some of these will be lower-performing funds, but they play a big role in a smart diversification strategy by managing unforeseen risk. Different types of funds will provide support when others perform poorly.

Nobody can look at a calendar and see that a bear market is coming. Anyone who tries to diversify into safe assets once the wrath of a bear market has struck will face sky-high bond prices, and equities that are worth peanuts. The average investor, left to his or her own devices and investing ignorance, will always sell low and buy high, thus producing the worst possible outcome. Market volatility almost always causes emotions to run high and investors to run for safety and sell at the wrong time.

Diversification is a powerful technique, but your employees should be reminded that they must accept the seemingly counterintuitive actions to achieve it. It's crucial that they understand and believe in the benefits now.

A final point about diversification: although risk can be mitigated by diversifying, risk is a reflection of constantly evolving business and economic cycles and each person's needs over time.

Put simply: risk changes over time. That's why rebalancing is so important.

REBALANCING

Rebalancing is the systematic process of reallocating the assets within a portfolio to keep each asset's share of the portfolio in line with predetermined percentages.

Employees may be thinking, "If stocks are doing better than bonds, what's the problem? Why would anyone want to sell the asset class that's going up and reinvest money in the one that's going down?"

They need to understand that winners often become losers. If an employee's winners now represent a higher percentage than he or she started with, then the risk exposure has increased. When that asset class turns negative, the employee may be poised for big losses and become unable to earn the desired rate of return, they need to achieve their income replacement ratio.

Auto rebalancing

Auto rebalancing a portfolio is one of the most psychologically difficult concepts for most employees to understand.

Employees should be investing in a diversified portfolio that over time will provide their *needs-based* rate of return to pay for all the things they want to do in their retirement years (see page 91 for more on needs-based rate of return).

Their investments should be allocated across different investment classes in different percentages to reduce overall risk. Over time, however, some investments will outperform others, and their asset allocation will stray from their original diversification strategy.

One significant way to reduce the straying effect is to rebalance the portfolio. How does this work? Well, let's say you started with an asset allocation strategy of 50% stocks and 50% bonds. If stocks do poorly and bonds do better, the value of these assets in the portfolio may move from 50/50 to, say 40/60. There is now a greater percentage of assets in bonds than the employee initially wanted. Over the long term, this may reduce returns if bonds underperform equities. On the other hand, equities may perform better than bonds over a long period of time, as was the case in the 1990s. If your employee's portfolio had become over-weighted with a high percentage of stock—say 90 percent—and a small percentage of bonds—10 percent—and the market drops 43 percent like it did from 2000 to 2002, they would feel the tragic impact of an unbalanced portfolio.

You may be thinking, "If that investment sector is going to do well, then why should they sell when they're making money?" The answer is twofold: (1) eventually, all markets turn, and when they do, they turn hard and fast; and (2) your employees are drifting away from the original guideposts they started investing with. If more and more capital ends up in one investment class, the risk exposure may increase, or, conversely, the portfolio may not be poised to earn a large enough return to meet their goals.

Buy low and sell high

Those five magic words once again sum it up: buy low and sell high. Rebalancing is the professional and systematic process that guarantees that your employees are always buying something relatively low with dollars they sold from something relatively high, and that's how they will increase their chances of success.

Reduce volatility

Automatic rebalancing over longer periods of time also reduces a portfolio's volatility. *Volatility* is the dramatic swing in a specific investment's returns. When an investment is up 50 percent and then drops 50 percent, that's a 100 percent swing in returns. Most studies show that annually rebalancing a portfolio to an investor's original asset allocation helps reduce the portfolio's volatility and provides smoother, steadier returns.

A valuable resource on this subject is Craig L. Israelsen, PhD. Dr. Israelsen is the developer of the 7Twelve Portfolio (www.7TwelvePortfolio.com). He has probably done more research on the benefits of automatic rebalancing than anyone I know. Every one of his studies continues to validate its benefits.

Take emotions out of the equation

When it comes to manual rebalancing, most people take the wait-and-see approach, but that will nearly guarantee they make the wrong decision. Why? When some funds outpace the market, they won't want to sell them. Those funds are how they're making money and they'll want to target the lower-performing funds as a drag on their success. Technology has to be the answer to take emotions out of the equation.

A word of caution about automatic investing

Automatic 401(k) investing provides enormous benefits, but there are also drawbacks. Using the automated process can make your employees complacent and overly confident. They still need to be involved in the process. Autopilot does not replace pilots. Instead, these features make the process easier.

Your plan participants need to set their goals, contribute to their goals, and stick with them. These automated processes won't automatically bring success, but they'll make some of the most important decisions easier and more consistent, and they'll limit the negative impact of emotions.

HOW FEES AFFECT PARTICIPANTS' RETURNS

A great deal has been written about fees in 401(k) plans. The Department of Labor, along with the news media, have put the spotlight on fees and expenses with something called 408(b)(2) and 404(a)(5) fee disclosure requirements. Employees have won multimillion-dollar lawsuits against large 401(k) plans that are focused on fees and what are called revenue-sharing arrangements by service providers of these retirement plans. (See *Tussey v. ABB*—Fiduciary Matters Blog.)

408(B)(2) FEE DISCLOSURE

It is the responsibility of the plan sponsor fiduciaries to 1) receive the full 408(b)(2) fee disclosure statements from their service providers (each year) and 2) understand ALL of the fees that are being charged to the plan and plan participants to make sure these fees are "reasonable."

The best way for the plan fiduciaries to know if their plan fees are "reasonable" is to regularly review and benchmark the fees that the retirement plan is paying.

However, when it comes to the actual plan investments, the Department of Labor has made it clear that cheaper is not necessarily better.

Let me give you a simple example. Which investment would you prefer: a large-cap growth fund, whose money manager has provided an average 6 percent annual return over the past 30 years, with a management fee of 0.50 percent (50 basis points), or a similar large-cap growth fund whose manager has provided an 8 percent average annual return for the past 30 years but charges 1 percent (100 basis points)—in other words, twice what the other one is charging? (For more information on basis points, please see section on basis points and expense ratios, page 73)

Most people would choose the manager with the lower fee, because they are focused on the cost and not on the total average annual return, the net of expenses. Instead, they should have invested with the manager with the higher management fee. If you look at the average annual return NET of fees, the manager who charged 1 percent generated a higher return of almost 1.5 percent a year, or $262,831 more over 30 years.

GROWTH OF $100,000 OVER 30 YEARS
EXPENSES CONSIDERED WITH PERFORMANCE

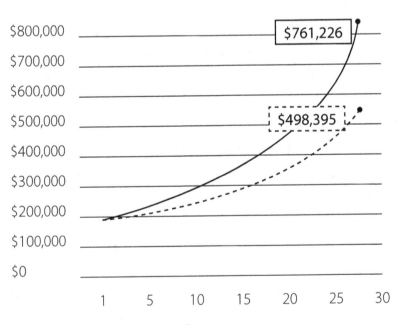

— 1% Expense/Net 7% Return

---- .50% Expense/Net 5.5% Return

This is a hypothetical example and not representative of any specific product.

The chart demonstrates the significant difference between these two managers impact on a participant account balance over a long period of time.

Much has been written about which is better in the long term: lower-cost index passive investing or active money management. In the arena of 401(k) plans, the judges in the major ERISA lawsuits, have given some guidance about offering a diversified investment line-up. The judges have commented that it is prudent to offer a 401(k) plan that provides employees the choice of both low-cost index funds and more expensive actively managed funds—provided the plan fiduciaries monitor the fees and investment returns on a regular basis and document the process.

In the final analysis, fees matter and so does performance. No one should overpay or overlook the impact fees can have on your employees' ability to meet their income replacement ratio needs at retirement and create a lifetime of income. Over long periods of time, excess fees can indeed erode your employees monthly retirement income.

The following chart illustrates the importance of managing the fees in your 401(k) plan for your employees' long-term retirement success.

IMPACT OF JUST FEES ON THE GROWTH
OF $100,000 OVER 30 YEARS

*Assumes a 6% return less the expense

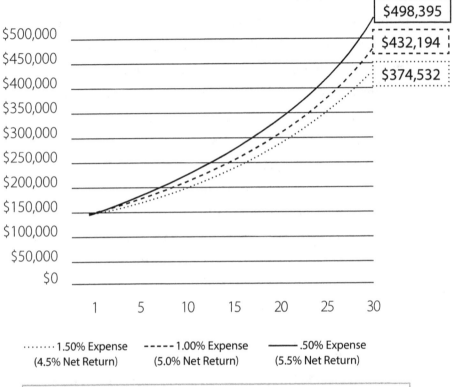

.... 1.50% Expense   ----- 1.00% Expense   —— .50% Expense
(4.5% Net Return)   (5.0% Net Return)   (5.5% Net Return)

WHAT DOES THIS MEAN FOR THEIR PAYCHECK FOR LIFE®?

Money at Retirement	Monthy Income	Total Income*
$498,395	$3,384/month	$812,160
$432,194	$2,948/month	$707,520
$374,532	$2,567/month	$616,080

*Total Income considers money at retirement plus a 20 year distribution phase (age 65-85) at which time a 6% Net Return is assumed. Fees, taxes, or other additional expenses are not factored into the distribution phase. Monthly income is derived by a division of twenty, 12 months periods (240) into Total Income.

This is a hypothetical example and not representative of any specific product.

This chart assumes an employee starts with an account balance of $100,000 which grows at a gross rate of return of 6%, compounded for 30 years. It shows the difference in the total accumulation over that period of time if your employee invested in a mutual fund that had a 1.50%, 1.00% or 0.50% average annual expense ratio.

Thereafter, I have calculated the amount of monthly income your employee could withdraw from each investment, from Age 65-85. I have assumed that their account value would continue to grow at 6% net of expenses over those 20 years.

Fees not only significantly affect the amount of money your employees will accumulate over their working years, but they also erode the amount of monthly income they may receive during their retirement years. The employee who invested in the fund with the lowest fee has $3,384 of monthly income or a total payout of $812,160 vs. the employee who paid the highest fees, has $2,567 of monthly income or $616,080 of total income. That is a difference of $817 a month or $196,080 of total "Paychecks for Life" over 20 years!

A prudently designed retirement plan is one that, in effect, says to the employees, "Look, for those of you who want low-cost index funds, we have them. For those of you who want active managers who might be able to out-perform the lower-cost index funds, you have that choice, too."

CONTROLLING FEES AND EXPENSES

As an employer, you can help your employees understand how they can make money by controlling fees and expenses.

The majority of 401(k) participants are not aware of all the costs involved in managing their money.

Understanding these costs is just as important as building a diversified investment strategy that takes advantage of dollar-cost averaging and automatic rebalancing. Your employees might have a great investment strategy, but what's the point if they are paying too much for it?

If you were to open a business today, you'd have to pay a wide variety of expenses, commonly known as "overhead." Normal company overhead costs can be broken down into two categories: (1) hard-dollar expenses, including rent, utilities, insurance, legal and accounting services, and other business expenses unrelated to employees; and (2) soft-dollar expenses for employee-related items, such as salaries, bonuses, medical insurance, sick leave, and Social Security.

All 401(k) plans also have hard- and soft-dollar expenses.

Hard-dollar expenses

Hard-dollar expenses are the fees charged to a 401(k) plan to cover the day-to-day operations of the plan. These expenses are usually not communicated to plan participants. They include the cost of keeping 401(k) plans in compliance with current ERISA and Department of Labor regulations. These costs are specifically known as plan administration, design, and compliance expenses.

These hard-dollar fees are typically paid for by the employer.

But there are exceptions to this rule. Some employers pay for these expenses out of the assets of the plan. That is, they're indirectly paid by plan participants, often without their knowledge.

Most 401(k) plans also offer individual services, such as loan and distribution provisions. Whenever employees use these services, they will probably have to pay one-time processing charges of $50 or $100. These fees usually aren't high, but employees need to understand the costs they'll incur before availing themselves of any individual services.

Soft-dollar expenses

A soft dollar expense is a payment made by one service provider to another service provider indirectly to cover plan expenses so the plan sponsor does not have to pay the expense directly. Soft-dollar fees cover a wide range of services, including record-keeping, website services, automated access to investment information, and customer education and advice services.

These expenses include investment management fees, 12b-1 fees, sub-transfer fees, and asset-based or wrap fees.

Let's break these expenses down individually.

Revenue-sharing fees

When a 401(k) plan uses share classes other than institutionally priced, there will typically be some percentage of the fund's revenue that is being paid to the record-keeper. As a Plan Fiduciary, it is your job to determine whether this revenue is "reasonable" and whether the record-keeper should be retaining all or a portion of this revenue sharing.

I like to explain that some of the revenue sharing that is paid by a mutual fund is similar to a slotting fee that the mutual fund company is paying to the record-keeper for being able to "slot" their funds on the platform[9]. It is similar to what the supermarket industry does today. Next time you are in a "super" supermarket (or even a Costco or Walmart), go to the cereal aisle and count the number of different boxes of cereal on the shelf. There are

---

9 It is important to note that these various forms of compensation are paid by mutual fund companies (and/or their affiliates - such as their distributing broker-dealers) for justifiable services provided by the entity receiving this compensation.

hundreds of brands and varieties of the same cereal. Why are they all there? (Certainly not for your 10-year-old's consumption.)

They are there for the supermarket chain's benefit. The supermarket is charging the cereal company a "slotting-fee" for placement on their shelves and access to their customers. These fees can run into the hundreds of thousands of dollars, just to get one box in the right place on the shelf! When the supermarket actually sells the cereal box, it may only earn a margin of 2–3 percent; the real money is in the slotting or placement fees.

The 401(k) platform (think Fidelity, Nationwide, etc.) is a supermarket shelf of mutual funds. Those mutual funds are looking for "placement" and "access" to 401(k) participants who will invest in their fund rather than someone else's fund. In return, the fund companies pay a slotting fee for that privilege. The real question in today's environment is who owns that revenue sharing: the record-keeper or the participants.

As the Plan Sponsor Fiduciary, you have the obligation to (1) identify these revenue-sharing payments; (2) determine if they are reasonable and necessary for the operation of the plan; and (3) if not, negotiate those fees to be either reduced or paid back to the plan. As we have already discussed, the best way to do this is to regularly benchmark all of the fees and expenses in your plan.

The following graphic represents potential fees that may be paid directly or indirectly by the fund to various service providers.

The total fees paid by the fund to the service provider may or may not exceed the total expense ratio of the actual mutual funds in your plan. For example, all of the compensation paid out may actually exceed the total annual mutual fund expense ratio that the shareholder bears.

POTENTIAL FEES, REVENUE SHARING AND EXPENSES OF A MUTUAL FUND

12b-1: Distribution expenses paid by mutual funds from fund assets. Includes commissions to brokers, marketing expenses and other administrative services.

Investment Management: Fees for managing investment assets. Charged as a percentage of the assets invested and deducted from the investment return.

Shareholder Servicing: Revenue shared by the mutual fund company with the service provider.

12b-1 Fees

Investment Management Fee

Shareholder Servicing Fees

Sub-TA (Agency Transfer Fees)

Asset/Wrap Fee: Additional fees layered on top of total investment fees.

Sub-TA: Brokerage firms and mutual funds often contract recordkeeping and other services related to participant shares to a third party called a sub-transfer agent.

Investment management fees

These are the fees charged by a mutual fund company to pay for the investment managers. The fees are charged as a percentage of the assets invested (such as 0.25 percent to 2 percent).

12b-1 fees

These are distribution expenses paid by mutual funds from fund assets. They include compensation to brokers, marketing expenses, and other administrative costs.

Sub-transfer fees

Brokerage firms and mutual funds often contract record-keeping and other services related to participant shares to a third party called a sub-transfer agent. The fee can be paid as a fixed fee on a per-participant basis, an asset-based fee, or a combination of both.

Asset-based or wrap fees

An asset fee or wrap fee is used by the record-keeper to recover costs and/or profits associated with managing the plan that are not being fully recovered by the mutual funds other revenue-sharing fee.

Plan consulting fees

These are the fees paid to a registered investment advisor, or consultant, or they can be commissions paid to the broker for the advisory services provided to the plan. The employer may pay them directly as a hard-dollar expense, or the employees may pay them indirectly as a soft-dollar expense deducted from the investment assets in each fund.

Mutual fund share classes defined

Let's look at an example of how revenue can be paid from a mutual fund depending on its "revenue" share class. The following table[10] shows a hypothetical mutual fund family with three different share classes.

R-6 Shares: If your 401(k) plan uses the R-6 share class, there is "zero" revenue sharing. This means your employees will pay the expense ratio of the fund which will cover the investment management cost as well as other expenses, (e.g. custodial, legal, transfer agent services, various administrative charges applicable to all share classes, etc.), which is equal to .50 percent. You, as the Plan Sponsor, absorb all the other plan costs (i.e., the administrative fees, including record-keeping, compliance and plan administration; and plan consulting fees, including advisor compensation and consulting fees).

R-4 Shares: If your plan uses the R-4 share class, there is 0.35 percent of revenue sharing. Your employees would pay for the investment management fee and the plan administration fees and you as the Plan Sponsor may absorb all other plan-related costs.

R-3 Shares: If your plan uses the R-3 share class, there is 0.65 percent of revenue sharing. In this case, your employees may absorb 100% of the cost of the plan operation, and you the plan sponsor may pay nothing.

---

10 This example is not necessarily typical of all mutual fund families. Some may only have 1 or 2 share classes available for use in a retirement plan. This example is being provided to show various revenue sharing arrangements.

SHARE CLASS MATTERS
ABC LARGE GROWTH FUND

Share Class	Year-to-Date Return	1-Year Return	3-Year Annualized Return	5-Year Annualized Return	Expense Ratio	Revenue Sharing
R3	19.79%	19.79%	7.05%	13.17%	1.14%	0.65%
R4	20.17%	20.17%	7.37%	13.50%	0.85%	0.35%
R6	20.58%	20.58%	7.74%	13.85%	0.50%	0.00%

These values do not actually reflect real results. We assumed a hypothetical gross return amount and then calculated the annualized returns based off the differing share classes' expense ratios. This illustration is meant to just demonstrate how the difference in share class can affect a fund's net returns.

Basis points and expense ratios

Each of those fund fees will most likely be reported in basis points (often abbreviated "bps"), where one basis point equals a hundredth of 1 percent (i.e., 100 basis points = 1 percent). A basis point just identifies all digits to the right hand side of the decimal in a percentage amount: If interest rates increase from 10 percent to 10.25 percent, they have increased by 25 basis points.

Why bother with basis points and not just stick with percentages? The financial industry uses them to avoid uncertainty. For example, if interest rates are 10 percent and are reported to have increased by 1 percent, you may be uncertain if they moved to 10.1 percent (a 1 percent relative increase) or 11 percent (an absolute gain of 1 percent). It's much clearer to use basis points. If interest rates of 10 percent are reported to have increased by 10 basis points, then there's no question they're now 10.1 percent.

The Securities and Exchange Commission (SEC) requires all funds to disclose both shareholder fees and operating expenses in a fund prospectus, a legal document your employees should receive for each fund in which they invest, and which they can access at any time from the 401(k) plan.

The prospectus provides material information about investment objectives, performance, risk, manager tenure, and more. In addition, the 401(k) website should have a simplified fund fact sheet for each investment, which will summarize all fund expenses.

404(a)(5) participant fee disclosure

To provide greater clarity and confidence for your employees, the Department of Labor (DOL) each year requires that your record keeper disclose all of the fees in the plan for your employees. Once a year, you as the employer are required to distribute this disclosure. In addition, all record keepers today post these fees on the website.

Not all fees are created equal: Bonds vs. stocks

In most cases, a given charge will be lower relative to a fund's return for a stock fund than a bond fund. For example, if a stock fund charges 100 basis points (1 percent) and returns 10 percent for the year, then the relative cost is 10 percent (1 percent / 10 percent) of the portfolio's returns.

Bond funds, on the other hand, because of the lower risk, are expected to have lower returns. If a bond fund charges the same 100 basis points but returns 5 percent, the relative cost is 20 percent (1 percent / 5 percent). Not only do your employees need to pay attention to the absolute cost (1 percent, in this example), but also the relative costs (10 percent and 20 percent, respectively).

Not all basis points are created equally; employees must consider them against the expected returns.

Active vs. passive management

Fees will also vary based on whether the fund is actively or passively managed.

Actively managed funds employ fund managers and research staffs who monitor performance. They constantly watch economic data and market valuations to determine whether they should buy, sell, or hold positions. Their goal, of course, is to outperform broad-based indexes such as the S&P 500.

Due to the additional time, staffing, and associated trading costs, actively managed funds will have higher fees than will their passively managed counterparts.

Passively managed accounts are run on autopilot, so there's no need for managers and research staffs. They're usually tied to an index, such as the S&P 500, which is easy to do. The fund simply buys the same securities in the same proportions as the index and then holds on. The fund mirrors the index and rises and falls with it, dollar for dollar. There's no daily monitoring, research, or heavy trading activity, so the fees tend to be significantly lower.

For passive funds, expense ratios may range from 10 to 25 bps (basis points) and for active funds, 65 to 250 bps.

Large vs. small funds

Another factor that drives a fund's expense ratio is the fund size. Usually, smaller funds and specialized funds (emerging markets or Internet technology, for example) are more expensive to operate; therefore, their expense ratios may be higher.

It's important to note that fund performance is always calculated after the expense ratio. If a fund earned 10 percent last year and had a 100 basis point (1 percent) expense ratio, the performance would be listed at 9 percent. That number is what is published in the prospectuses and websites that track mutual fund performances.

SAVE AMERICA SAVE ACTION STEPS

1. Understanding your role as a 401(k) Plan Fiduciary is critical to managing a successful retirement plan.

2. Be sure you do a full vendor benchmarking of all your service providers every three to five years and document your process. This will aid you in determining if the fees you are paying are reasonable and the services and investment choices you have are optimal for your employees to achieve a successful retirement outcome. A retirement plan specialist consultant is a valuable advisor to assist you in managing this process.

3. Your 401(k) should offer a diversified fund line-up of 16–18 alternative investment options, both active and low-cost passive investments. Limit their choices—more options than that may confuse your employees enough so that they choose not to participate in the plan at all.

4. A well-managed target date fund or managed account is an ideal choice for 85 percent of your employees. Be sure you have a process for evaluating and monitoring your target date fund or managed account. Document this process.

ACTION STEPS CONTINUED

5. Investment Due Diligence: Be certain to have a disciplined investment due diligence process for hiring, monitoring, and replacing all investment choices in your plan. This can be conducted by a skilled retirement advisor who specializes in this industry. The analysis should be separate from any reporting provided by your 401(k) record keeper, so it is independent. This process should be provided quarterly, semi-annually, or annually, depending on your plan size. The process should be documented to meet your fiduciary obligations.

6. Fees can greatly impact your employees ability to adequately meet their income replacement ratio goals.

7. As a fiduciary, it is your obligation and responsibility to understand:

   ▫ Who your service providers are

   ▫ The services they provide

   ▫ Whether those services are necessary for the plan

   ▫ All of the fees your service providers receive, both hard and soft dollar compensation

   ▫ If the fees are reasonable

   ▫ If a service provider is acting as a fiduciary to the plan

   ▫ If they have any conflicts of interest

PART FOUR

CREATING SMART SAVERS

EDUCATION IS KEY TO MOTIVATING EMPLOYEES

What else can you do to help your employees prepare for a successful retirement? Let's say you have implemented your courageous plan design and have taken advantage of all the Auto[5] design features. You have made available a robust investment lineup of active and low-cost passive investments. You offer a well-managed target-date fund. You meet your fiduciary obligations of monitoring and benchmarking plan investments and fees. Is that enough?

Not necessarily. You should also consider educating your employees on the benefits of participating in their 401(k) Plan. We believe regular, robust employee education is a key ingredient to getting employees engaged, getting them motivated to save more on an incremental basis, and getting them to stay fully engaged in saving and investing.

Remember, even with Auto[5], employees can still opt out. If all you did was Auto[5], and everybody said "no," then you have failed to get your employees engaged and taking full responsibility for their retirement.

Employers need to offer both group education meetings and individual one-on-one meetings. These meetings must be customized to the plan demographics and employees' education level.

If you have an engineering firm or a firm with a lot of Ph.D.s, you definitely want to provide education that speaks to that level. But if you have a hotel chain of hourly workers who may only have a high school education, you need to be sensitive to their level of understanding.

You don't want to talk over their heads. You want to make things simple to understand and keep people engaged at every level. I have seen too many "canned" 401(k) investment meetings that put employees to sleep or just frustrated them by talking over their "listening level."

THE 'PAYCHECKS FOR LIFE' PRINCIPLES

When teaching investment and saving strategies to employees, we reference a wide variety of educational material, including the following books from respected industry authors: *Save More Tomorrow: Practical Behavioral Finance Solutions to Improve 401(k) Plans,* by Shlomo Benartzi; *Transform Tomorrow: Awakening the Super Saver in Pursuit of Retirement Readiness,* by Stig Nybo and Liz Alexander; and *Paychecks for Life: How to Turn Your 401(k) into a Paycheck Manufacturing Company,* by Charles D. Epstein.

We use the nine Paycheck for Life Principles from *Paychecks for Life* to teach employees how to take responsibility for saving and investing wisely to meet their income replacement ratio goal at their retirements.

It's an engaging process that gets employees excited about saving and investing for their retirement years. We typically teach these principles through a series of group meetings. These can be done quarterly, semi-annually, or annually, depending on the needs and requirements of our clients.

Based on the plan-level metrics we obtain, we offer customized one-on-one meetings for all plan participants. They're not mandatory, but on a voluntary basis. What we find is that when we teach the Paychecks for Life Principles, employees get interested and excited enough to voluntarily sign up for our one-on-one meetings. We require our plan sponsors to make time during the work week for us to meet with their employees.

We've learned in our 35 years in business that participants will take action when we are able to meet with them one-on-one and personalize these educational meetings to their financial concerns, goals, and objectives. They will increase their savings rate, adjust their investment allocation, and make progress toward their income replacement ratio number.

Personal gap statements

For each employee who meets with us, we provide a personalized "gap" statement[11]. Let me describe what that is. We create a customized paycheck report that shows employees what would happen to their weekly paycheck if they were to increase their 401(k) contribution by 1 percent, 2 percent, 3 percent or more. It not only gives them the net tax savings and the net cost to their paycheck, but it also shows them how much money they'll accumulate at retirement, based on a reasonable rate of return, and converts that amount into a hypothetical monthly income.

11 Gap statements are hypothetical in nature and use assumptions that may not be achieved.

Once an employee sees this personal gap report that shows them how much money they could potentially have by saving 1 percent, 2 percent, 3 percent or more, they begin to realize how small increases in their contribution rate can potentially impact the amount of money they could have for retirement. The gap report hypothetically shows them how much money they need to save to have enough money to pay for all the things they want to do at retirement, versus how much they're saving now. It's further reinforcement of why they need to increase their savings rate and the power of compound interest over time, and the importance of proper asset allocation of their investment choices.

> If you would like an example of our Employee Gap Statement, you can e-mail us at info@epsteinfinancial.com and simply say, "Please send me a sample Employee Gap Statement."

We follow the Department of Labor's Interpretive Bulletin 96-1; Participant Investment Education; Final Rule (06/11/1996), which provides a road map on how best to provide investment education to plan participants.

In the pages ahead, I will explain the concept of "Desirement Mortgage®" and tell you about a calculator that will help your employees prepare for their future. You will find that free calculator on the website www.paychecksforlife.org.

THREE STAGES OF INVESTMENT LIFE

Your employees may love their jobs, but it is human nature to dream about how they will use their time someday when they don't have to work. Those are the years when they should be able to devote themselves to all the things they dreamed about doing—or what I call their "desirements."

Instead of using the words "retirement years," therefore, I am choosing to call them the "desirement years." Doesn't that sound better? One definition of retirement is "to put out of use." I don't know anyone who wants to be put out of use when they retire. Most everyone I speak to is looking forward to doing all the things they desire to do in life.

In fact, when we talk to employees about it, we call it "Desirement Planning®." Desirement planning, in short, is helping employees figure out how much money they need to pay for all the things they "desire" to do when they retire.

We use the desirement concept in explaining to employees the three stages of one's investment life and how their perspective on risk is likely to change as they get older. The following is what your employees need to know about those three distinct stages of investing.

Earning Years	Squirreling Years	Desirement Years
Accumulate	Protect	Spend
Ages 21 to 54	Ages 55 to 64	Ages 65 to life expectancy

Earning years

The primary earning years usually last from ages 21 to 54 (though they may start earlier or go later, depending on when people choose to start or stop working). These are the years when they need to accumulate money. The sooner they start, the sooner compound interest will go to work for them. Those dollars are ready to work 24/7/365, through good markets and bad, with one purpose: to create those Paychecks for Life.

Squirreling years

From ages 55 to 64, investors should protect an increasing percentage of their capital from the effects of bear markets that might occur at the beginning of their desirement years. They want to reduce their exposure to riskier investments in their 401(k) and move into safer havens, such as bonds or cash equivalents.

The key thing to understand here is that a bear market can last three to six years and can represent a loss of 20 percent or more of the value of the investments. To protect this value, investors in this age range should move an increasing percentage of their money into more conservative bonds and cash equivalents, until they have accumulated enough reserve money to cover the cost of three to five years of income needs.

Desirement years

At this stage, typically age 65, the investment strategy should be to protect hard-earned capital and generate income. The goal is to earn a needs-based rate of return equal to or slightly higher than taxes and inflation, which should be a very conservative 5 percent to 7 percent.

THE DESIREMENT PLANNING® PROCESS

"You have to believe your future is bigger than your past."

We encourage your employees to think like entrepreneurs. They need to have a deep-seated belief that their future is bigger than their past. They consistently plan and dream about what the future can and will look like. They believe wholeheartedly that if they set specific goals, actually write them down, and fine-tune them on a weekly, monthly, quarterly, and annual basis, that they'll be successful in creating a future that's much more fulfilling than their past. This is the entrepreneurial spirit, and it should be fully embraced.

As you help your employees with their investment goals, you may encounter an attitude of helplessness. Some may be thinking, "Who, me? I can't do that! Do you have any idea what my circumstances are? My income is not that high, and I have too much debt." My answer to that is that we all have specific circumstances in our lives that might seem like barriers to our aspirations; focusing solely on these will certainly limit our ability to be more successful and achieve our dreams. We must not let the past dictate our future. We need to start writing down our dreams and goals for our desirement years. We need to believe that the future will be greater than the past, that what lies ahead is bigger and better.

The Desirement Planning Process puts your employees on course toward securing a financial future with reduced anxiety. The process involves two critical steps for calculating the cost of their retirement (desirement) years and for creating a financial mechanism for covering these costs long after the paychecks have stopped.

Step one: creating a desirement wish list

We encourage your employees to imagine all of the things they have dreamed about doing someday, when they are no longer working. They should make a list of the exotic places they have always wanted to visit, the second home they would love to build or buy, that cruise they have always wanted to take to some exotic island, those recreational activities—sailing, fishing, hunting, skiing, mountain climbing, hiking, parachuting—that they have long desired to try.

Some may want to go back to school or teach, become active in charities that could use their help, plant the garden they have always wanted, renovate the house, read all the books waiting on the shelf, or just spend more time with the grandchildren. The possibilities are endless.

This is their Desirement Wish List for their brighter future, and they will add to it throughout their working years. It represents their desirements for what they will do in their retirement.

Step two: calculating a desirement number

The next step is to put a price tag on all the wonderful things they want to do and to have in their desirement years. These can be broken down into:

1. Fixed expenses, such as house costs, taxes, and utilities

2. Desirement costs (or what we call Desirement expenses), such as travel, schooling, one-time purchases, etc.

At this point, your employees may be thinking that they can barely calculate and budget their current expenses—so how can they be expected to figure out what something is going to cost in 20, 30, or possibly 40 years?

True, it's a difficult task. If an employee does not wish to create their desirement wish list, then they can simply use the income replacement formula that we discussed earlier in this book and determine if they want to try to replace 70 percent, 80 percent, or 90 percent of their current income adjusted for inflation. Your current 401(k) record-keeping website should have an income replacement calculator for your employees to use.

THE DESIREMENT MORTGAGE CALCULATOR[12]

To determine the amount of money an employee needs to save to finance his or her desirement years, we use The 401k Coach Desirement Mortgage® Calculator. It is based on the same principles as when someone buys a home and takes out a mortgage.

Many of your employees will certainly relate to that, and that's a good way to help them understand the principles involved. When a homebuyer seeks financing, he or she may go to the bank to take out a mortgage for that purchase price, perhaps for 30 years at a fixed rate. That same idea can apply to financing one's desirement years. Think of it as a Desirement Mortgage. The amount financed is the Desirement Mortgage Number. How much does the employee need to "pay" (save) each month to accumulate the target amount?

If your employees were like most first-time homebuyers, they worried about how they were going to come up with the down payment for that home and then how they would make the mortgage payment each month. But after they purchased that house and made some adjustments in their monthly budget, they found that making the monthly mortgage payment wasn't so hard after all. They were able to make the payment no matter what, through good stock markets and bad, through one child to seven.

It all worked out. Why? It worked because they made a commitment to something they really wanted, something they desired, something they would own (and finance) for at least 30 years.

12 The Desirement Mortgage Calculator is not a mortgage calculator, but rather a calculator that will help you estimate what percentage of your income you may need to save each pay period into your 401(k) to generate an adequate income when you stop working to pay for all the things you "desire" to do. You can find the calculator at www.paychecksforlife.org.

What was it that helped make their dream of homeownership a reality? Unconsciously, they had a formula for success that allowed them to achieve that dream.

The homeownership formula for success probably looked something like this:

1. They identified their dream house and what it would cost.

2. They committed to paying for that dream house within a certain period of time.

3. They calculated what it would cost, i.e. what they could afford to finance each month as a mortgage payment.

4. They saved for the down payment.

5. They adjusted their plan and budget to overcome unforeseen financial obstacles that might prevent them from achieving the dream of homeownership.

6. They never stopped believing that they could save for and finance their goal of homeownership.

7. They achieved their dream—their "desirement"—and purchased that first home.

Now, compare that with another success formula—the one for their "desirement years" mortgage.

1. They create their desirement wish list and calculated the desirement number for what it would cost.

2. They commit to funding their desirement years in a certain period of time.

3. They calculate what it would cost each month to make their desirement "mortgage" payment.

4. They calculate their down payment; i.e., what Social Security and any current retirement assets, such as 401(k)s and IRAs, would be worth in their desirement years.

5. They adjust their plan and budget to overcome unforeseen financial obstacles that might prevent them from achieving their dream of having a paycheck for life to fund their desirement years.

6. They never stop believing they could save for and finance their goal of a financially secure desirement.

7. They succeed in funding their desirement mortgage and are generating Paychecks for Life in their desirement years.

The Desirement Mortgage Calculator will help calculate how much money your employees must save each month with the least amount of risk to generate enough money to pay for all the things they desire to do when they retire.

To drive these concepts home, let's imagine that you have an employee with the following details:

1. Current age: 35

2. Desirement age: 65

3. Needs-based rate of return: 6 percent

4. Current annual income: $40,000

5. Annual raise (inflation): 3 percent

6. Annual Social Security income at retirement: $0

7. Desired percentage of income in retirement: 70 percent ($28,000 annually before inflation)

The desirement number is $1,209,652.

Now, if that same employee had $15,000 in annual Social Security as part of the down payment, the desirement number is reduced to $967,950.

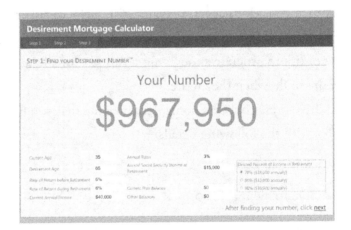

If she has $45,000 in current retirement savings (current plan balance), your employee's desirement number shrinks to $696,934.

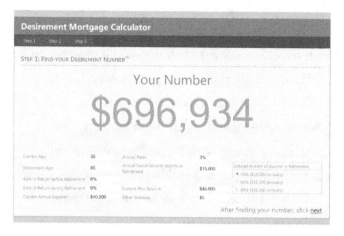

Here's something else that's amazing about this desirement mortgage calculator. What I have found to be true—and this is from talking to people who make $20,000 a year, to people who make $500,000—is that whatever their mortgage payment is on their house, that monthly amount is almost exactly what they will need to save each month in their 401(k) to have enough money to pay for all the things they will desire to do in their "desirement years," with the least amount of risk!

In other words, if someone's mortgage payment was $500 a month, he or she would need to save somewhere around $500 a month in the 401(k) plan. If the mortgage payment was $3,000 a month, then $3,000 a month is the desirement mortgage number.

NEEDS-BASED VS. GREED-BASED RETURNS

If you were to ask employees how much they want to earn on their money every year in their 401(k), what would you expect them to say? At group meetings, they'll shout out, 15 percent, 20 percent, 30 percent, even 100 percent.

Investing behaviors of participants and their return expectations are unrealistic. The desire to earn such high rates of return is unsustainable over time. Some employees are basically gambling with their retirement savings, because they end up choosing investments that have far more risk than they could possibly understand. Again, that's why I say the 401(k) plan is America's largest casino.

In 2008, when the "credit crisis" hit the equity markets, 401(k) participants got hit with 30–45 percent losses[13] in their account balances. Many employees jumped out of the market into cash at the bottom, and still haven't gotten back into a well-diversified portfolio, which is a shame because those same equity markets have recovered over the last six years.

Employees investing in a 401(k) plan typically tend to take more risk than is necessary, because they don't know the most important number when it comes to investing for their retirement. It's called their needs-based rate of return.

A person's needs-based rate of return is the rate they need to earn on their retirement assets year in and year out with the least amount of risk to ensure they have enough money to generate a Paycheck for Life throughout their retirement.

By contrast, the greed-based rate of return is what employees are seeking when they tell you that the amount they want to earn on their investments is "as much as I can get!" That attitude can have major consequences on how they manage the money that they invest for their desirement mortgage. It's what causes the average 401(k) investor to pick investments that have done well in the past, forgetting that historic performance is no guarantee of what will happen in the future. It is what caused millions of 401(k) investors to take undue risk with their investment choices and lose 40 percent

13 S&P 500 Index McGraw Hill Financial 2008 Annual Performance

or more of their value in 2009 (if they had been invested primarily in the 500 U.S. largest stocks, i.e., the S&P 500)[14], and then blame their 401(k) for those results. The 401(k) wasn't to blame; investor greed and lack of proper management were.

The greed-based rate is what causes people to treat their 401(k) plan like a casino, rather than like their home. Would you go to a casino, right now, and bet your house on "red number nine" at the roulette table? How about the craps table, "lucky seven?" Of course not.

But that's exactly what millions of Americans do every day when they attempt to pick the investments in a 401(k) plan without knowing the needs-based rate of return. I can't begin in these pages to make everyone a savvy investor (as opposed to a crafty gambler); nor do I want to. What I can do is show investors how to be intelligent entrepreneurs and stewards of their investments—by treating that money with the same care and respect that they give their home and their mortgage. Those who do so will have a better chance of arriving at their desirement years with two very secure assets: a home that is fully paid off, and a 401(k) potentially filled with enough dollars to generate Paychecks for Life.

The opinion of financial advisors and economic pundits across America varies widely as to what is a reasonable and safe rate of return that the average worker needs to earn on their retirement assets to adequately replace their working income throughout their retirement years. It is the opinion of this author, that the needs-based rate of return for the average worker is between 4 percent and 6 percent. That's it. The exact rate depends on a number of variables, including the years they have until retirement, the amount of savings they currently have, and their desired amount of future income.

14 S&P 500 Index McGraw Hill Financial, 1 year performance as of 02/2009

To put this 4 percent to 6 percent desirement mortgage rate in perspective, someone establishing a simple cash balance pension plan today, which is a conservative retirement plan, would have to hire an actuary to calculate how much savings would be needed to achieve a guaranteed amount of money at retirement. In making this calculation, the actuary would assume that the money could be invested at a conservative rate of return of 5.1 percent to 5.5 percent.

By applying that pension-plan rate of return to their 401(k), your employees increase the potential chances that their plan will accumulate enough funds to generate Paychecks for Life. That prevents them from gambling with their future.

To be successful entrepreneurs and stewards of their investments, your employees must generate enough return on their money with the least amount of risk to generate those Paychecks for Life. This means they must first calculate their needs-based rate of return before investing any money in their 401(k). They must resist investing for a greed-based rate of return. They can leave that kind of thrill for a trip to the casino.

Your employees must not be drawn in by the potential for high returns on investments that they do not understand and cannot afford to lose. You can show them far better ways to enhance their performance and reduce their desirement mortgage payment.

For example, they can use "OPM"—Other People's Money— in their investments to reduce that monthly payment by 50 percent or more. In the next section, I will explain how that will help your employees to understand this crucial concept.

OTHER PEOPLE'S MONEY (OPM)

Even if you're new to investing, you are probably familiar with the acronym OPM—Other People's Money. It's a common mantra in finance and even made for a great movie title starring Gregory Peck and Danny DeVito. On the more serious side, it was also the title of a collection of essays on the power of banks and financial institutions published in 1914 by Louis Brandeis, who later became one of the most influential members of the U.S. Supreme Court.

Whether used in a comedy movie or an essay to sway legal views, OPM combines two simple ideas: (1) it takes money to make money; and (2) if you don't have money, get it from other people. It's simple, but the effects are profound.

All financial institutions capitalize on OPM. Banks lend it. Publicly traded companies borrow it. Mutual funds invest it. Of course, the government spends it. And then there's Bernie Madoff, who simply stole it. The common thread is that all of them would rather risk somebody else's money rather than their own. Without OPM, opportunities are limited. With OPM, opportunities increase exponentially.

How banks use OPM: The multiplier effect

Take a bank, for instance. How does a bank make money? Most people never give this a second thought. They just assume that banks have a lot of money that they lend to others, but bankers are masters at using OPM and have taken it to a whole new level. They not only lend OPM, but they also lend money that doesn't even exist. How is that possible?

A bank attracts capital—OPM—by paying interest on cash balances. It then turns around and lends that cash to other people at higher interest rates. Simply put, banks take money from those who do not need it now (depositors) and transfers it to those who do (borrowers) to maximize the value of OPM.

Many people believe that 100 percent of their cash deposits are locked away tightly in a personalized vault; the truth is that only a small fraction stays with the bank, and none of it stays in personal accounts. Although funds are available if you should write a check or withdraw cash from an ATM machine, your deposits are immediately put to use in the bank's favor. If you do demand your money, the bank gets it, of course, from other people.

Banks are able to lend nearly all of people's deposits and shuffle funds from clients who do not immediately need the money to those who do because they operate on a *fractional reserve system*, which means they're required to keep only a fraction of deposits on reserve.

For each deposit made, only a small fraction, called the reserve requirement, is held in the bank's vault. The balance becomes available for loans. The reserve requirement is set by the Federal Reserve and is usually 10 percent or less. Although the requirement can be changed, it generally remains steady from year to year.

At this point, your employees may be saying, "Wait a minute, this sounds like marginal (or fractional, in this case) thinking"— and, *By George!*, that means the entrepreneurial bug is starting to catch on.

Let's trace a simple bank deposit and see OPM in action. Assume a client deposits $100 with a bank. The bank holds 10 percent, or $10, as the required reserve and lends the remaining $90 to another customer, who may deposit it with another bank. That bank, in turn, holds 10 percent, or $9, and lends the remaining $81. The process continues, but eventually must stop since each bank receives 10 percent less than the previous bank.

The initial $100 deposit has, therefore, created money that doesn't even exist. How much?

It turns out that if the reserve requirement is 10 percent, banks create an amount of money equal to one divided by the reserve requirement, or 1/0.10, which equals 10 times the amount of printed money. The $100 deposit is, therefore, expanded to $1,000. From a simple $100 deposit, $900 of additional money that never existed before is suddenly created—for other people to borrow.

If it sounds like a potentially unstable system, you're right. That is exactly why many banks became insolvent during the 1930s when many "runs on the bank" occurred. If depositors believe that a bank is in financial trouble, they may all rush to the bank to withdraw their money, which, in turn, raises the risk of bank default, thus causing more people to withdraw money. A run on a bank is a psychological, self-perpetuating event. In other words, the banking system is stable as long as everyone believes that it is.

Today, many systems are in place to prevent such bank runs. The Federal Deposit Insurance Corporation (FDIC) insures each depositor up to $250,000 in the event of a bank failure. As long as a customer does not have more than $250,000 in cash deposited with the bank, he or she would have no incentive to withdraw that money even if others were withdrawing theirs.

In addition, the Federal Reserve ("the Fed") acts as the "bankers' bank," ready, willing, and able to lend money to troubled banks in the event of bank panics. During the credit crisis of 2008, we witnessed the sheer leveraging power of the Federal Reserve. During one of the worst financial meltdowns since the Great Depression, the Fed created (printed) $700 billion in TARP (Troubled Asset Relief Program) funds, which it lent to the nation's largest banks to stimulate new bank lending and avoid a global run on the banking system. The more money in the banking system, the less chance of additional financial institution failure. Doing so restored confidence and faith in the financial system and markets.

So what's the point to understand from all of this? Banks make big money by taking OPM to another level—by lending money they don't even have. They have to do this to survive. Banks collect many short-term deposits but they make long-term loans, which creates a mismatch between their assets and liabilities.

Without OPM, it's enormously difficult to invest efficiently. All forms of successful businesses, big and small, understand the importance of OPM. It's the only way they compete and survive.

Your employees, too, must make OPM part of their plan if they wish to create a steady stream of Paychecks for Life. Without OPM, they would have to invest their own money and earn all of the invested funds themselves. It would be a slow process. They need to understand how much faster their 401(k)s will grow if they have access to OPM.

"And so, who are the other people who will give me money?" your employees will wonder. They actually have two partners who are willing and able to invest capital—OPM— with them: One is Uncle Sam. The other is you, the employer.

Partner #1: Uncle Sam's Money (USM)

If your employees were to take a dollar out of their wallets and each tear away a fourth of it, they would see immediately and graphically what happens to them if they are in the 25 percent tax bracket. Uncle Sam lays claim to one-quarter of each dollar earned.

What does Uncle Sam do with that 25 cents? He builds bridges and schools, manufactures airplanes and guns, provides agricultural programs, funds Medicaid, and so on—whatever he wants. Does he ever plan on giving it back to you once he's taken it? No. To the individual, that's 25 cents never to be seen again.

UNCLE SAM'S TAKE

What You Get

What Uncle Sam Gets

For investors, the problem is that they have also lost the interest that they could have earned on that quarter.

To those who say that doesn't sound like a lot, let me ask this: Suppose I were to give you one penny of that 25 cents, and you could double that penny every day for 30 days. How much money would you have at the end of that month? Ready for the answer?

$5,368,709.12

That's right: One penny compounded every day for a month equals $5,368,709.12.

What your employees need to understand is this: Uncle Sam is giving them a choice. They can either invest 100 percent of their dollar in their 401(k), or else they can give him 25 cents and put just 75 cents in their pocket to spend.

Guaranteed 33 Percent Return

Let's look at it another way. Let's assume that the employee earns $100 and is in the 25 percent tax bracket. She could pay the taxes and take $75 home to spend. On the other hand, if she decides to invest the $100 in a 401(k), she is not taxed on that money—at least not yet. The tax comes when she eventually withdraws the funds. The point is that the entire $100 contribution to the plan will begin working today.

By choosing to invest in a 401(k), the employee has an additional $25 that would not have been available by taking the $75 on an after-tax basis. That extra $25 would have been Uncle Sam's Money (USM) in the form of taxes. Those additional dollars represent a guaranteed 33 percent return on the money you have available to invest ($25 / $75). That alone should get people's attention.

Interest-free loan

Another way to look at USM is that it really is an interest-free loan. Where else can anyone get a 33 percent return? From the local bank? Hardly. In 2014, interest rates were a miserly 0.50 percent to 1.50 percent.

Successful entrepreneurs are always looking for OPM to borrow at the lowest rate possible. Well, USM is interest free! Investors may wonder, "What's the catch? What's my obligation for this interest-free USM?"

There are only two conditions. One, the money must remain working in the plan until the participant is 59.5 years old, at which point she can begin to withdraw funds without a 10 percent early withdrawal penalty. While participants are not required to pay any interest on the use of this money until then, they will be required to pay taxes when they withdraw it to generate their Paychecks for Life. The taxes that they pay will be based on the prevailing tax rates during their desirement years.

Second, when they reach the age of 70.5 and retire from the company, Uncle Sam requires that they begin withdrawing a minimum amount each year. Why? Because Uncle Sam wants to begin getting repaid for the money he has allowed the participant to use, interest-free, all those years. In essence, USM is a demand note or IOU that starts to become due at age 70.5 at the latest. A CPA or financial advisor can assist participants in making that calculation each year.

A word of caution: Many people believe that when they reach their desirement years they'll be in a lower tax bracket because their income will be lower. Let me put this myth to rest. The truth is that no one knows what tax bracket they will be in when they stop working, including the government. In their desirement years, people could actually be in a higher tax bracket than they are now, if Congress votes to raise the income tax rates.

Partner #2: Employer's Money (EM)

As part of your matching contribution, you the employer may also want to invest capital in your employees' 401(k) plan. The government also calls this investment a profit-sharing contribution or safe harbor contribution. For the employee, the bottom line is this: Such a contribution is another opportunity to invest using OPM.

Let's assume that you match the first 4 percent (under your Safe Harbor Design) of the income that the employee contributes. What this means is that the employee earns a 100 percent return on that 4 percent—instantly (depending on your company's vesting schedule). That's a remarkable return considering that the risk-free interest rate today is less than 1 percent per year and that the largest publicly traded corporations are proud to report a 20 percent return on assets at their annual shareholder meetings.

The 401(k) participants need to understand that this contribution of Employer's Money (EM) generates a consistent return of up to 100 percent on some of their investment dollars, and it's risk free and interest free.

Vesting

Depending on the design of the 401(k) plan, the matching contribution either automatically becomes the employees' money—which is known as 100 percent vested—or, more typically, it will become theirs gradually, beginning with 0 percent in the first year and increasing in increments of 20 percent per year over the next five years. At the end of six years, all of the money that you, the employer, have invested remains inside the 401(k), even if the employee leaves your company.

The USM/EM Multiplier Effect

Now let's look at the power of USM and EM combined. Let's assume you will match half of the first 6 percent of the income that the employees contribute. This means that on the first 6 percent of their pay, you will match 3 percent. Let's also assume that the employees are in a 25 percent federal tax bracket.

Suppose 6 percent of that pay equals $100 and an employee decides to contribute that full amount. Uncle Sam has actually lent the employee, interest free, $25 of that amount.

Employees who do so have, therefore, invested $75 of their own money and $25 of USM. Meanwhile, as the employer, you will match 50 percent of that contribution, or $50.

The employee now has $150 working in his 401(k) instead of $75 to spend. He has immediately doubled the money without even putting it into any investment. This is a risk-free rate to be found nowhere else. The higher the employee's tax bracket, the more valuable the effect of USM and EM.

OPM and the Desirement Mortgage concept

Let's combine what we learned about OPM and Desirement Mortgages. To do so, we'll use the Desirement Mortgage Calculator again. (Go to www. paychecksforlife.org and click on Desirement Mortgage Calculator.)

Let's continue to use the employee example from earlier in this chapter. She has the following details:

1. Current age: 35

2. Desirement age: 65

3. Needs-based rate of return: 6 percent

4. Annual income: $40,000

5. Annual raise (inflation): 3 percent

6. Annual Social Security income: $15,000

7. Desired percentage of income at retirement: 70 percent ($28,000 annually before inflation)

8. Current plan balance: $45,000

Based on these assumptions, she has a desirement number of $696,935.

Going to Step 2 of the calculator, Funding Your Number, shows her monthly mortgage payment is $690.

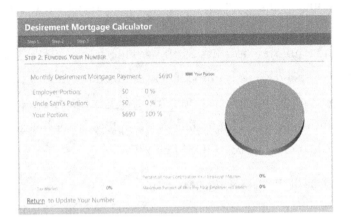

Uncle Sam's Money = OPM

If your employees make contributions to the 401(k) plan on a pre-tax basis, Uncle Sam will fund a percentage of their contributions equal to their tax bracket. In this case, we're assuming the 35-year-old is in a 25 percent federal tax bracket, which means Uncle Sam is paying $172 per month of her Desirement Mortgage payment, or 25 percent of the monthly payment.

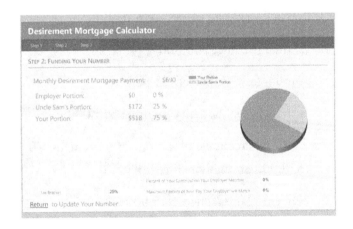

Company Contributions (OPM)

Any company contributions will help fund an employee's Desirement Mortgage payment. If you match 50 cents of every dollar that your employee contributes up to the first 6 percent, you would effectively contribute $100 per month to their Desirement Mortgage payment, or 14 percent of the entire monthly payment, in this employee example.

In the Desirement Mortgage Calculator, your employee would enter 50 percent for the Percent Your Employer Matches and 6 percent for the Maximum Percent Your Employer Matches.

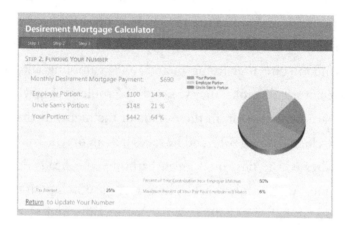

The Magic of OPM

In this example, OPM has reduced your 35-year-old employee's Desirement Mortgage by 35 percent, from $690 per month to $442 per month. That's lower than the average home mortgage payment! On a weekly basis, it's $102 per week or $14.50 per day.

You can input a real-life situation of your own by inserting the right variables into The Desirement Mortgage Calculator at www. paychecksforlife.org.

THE GREEN BATHROBE EFFECT

It's important that your employees are aware of a common mental accounting trap before they get started. Many 401(k) participants tend to think that because they have access to OPM, they should take unnecessary risks. After all, if it's not their money, why not roll the dice and reach their desirement goals even earlier?

Gary Belsky and Thomas Gilovich explain why that thinking is a critical mistake in their book *Why Smart People Make Big Money Mistakes and How to Correct Them*. They illustrate their point with an urban legend often told near Las Vegas casinos: "The Legend of the Man in the Green Bathrobe." Whether gamblers believe the story or not, it makes a cautionary point about OPM.

The story goes like this. A newlywed couple returns to their honeymoon suite after losing their $1,000 gambling allowance. They're not totally broke; they've saved a $5 roulette chip with #17 on its face as a souvenir. In the middle of the night, the husband sees the clock flashing 3:17 and he takes it as an omen. Too frantic to get dressed, he puts on a green bathrobe and heads down to the casino. At the roulette table, he places the $5 chip on #17, of course. Magically, the ball lands on that number and he collects 35 times his bet, or $175.

He takes the $175 winnings and bets it all on #17. The wheel spins and the ball miraculously lands there again. His winnings increase to $6,125. He does this again and again until he's worth $262 million.

He takes the $262 million and bets it all on his shockingly successful number #17. This time, though, Lady Luck deserts him. The ball lands on #18 and the man loses everything. With dampened spirits, he walks back to his hotel room.

"Where were you?" asks the bride.

"Playing roulette," he replies.

"How did you do?"

"Not bad. I only lost $5."

While the story makes a strong point in a humorous and exaggerated way, think seriously about where the error lies. While the groom's accounting methods may be acceptable for government use, I hope you agree that his loss was far more than $5. Even though he leveraged his money into $262 million doesn't mean that it had no value. Believing those millions have no value (or less value) is called a *mental accounting trap*.

While most investors agree that $5 is not his total loss, they make identical accounting errors with investing. For some reason, investors often feel that some dollars are worth more because of where they come from. They treat their own dollars with respect, but OPM dollars as free money. Don't fall for that. Just because other people contribute money to your 401(k) plan, doesn't mean their money isn't real.

Other people's money is real. If you treat it as anything less, I'll send you a green bathrobe.

SAVE AMERICA SAVE ACTION STEPS

1. Education is key to helping your employees understand their responsibility in saving for their "desirement years" and having a Paycheck for Life®.

2. A gap statement is a powerful tool for illustrating to an employee how incremental adjustments in "payroll deductions" to their 401(k) plan can reduce their current taxes and increase the monthly income they will have at retirement. Most 401(k) record keepers offer these "customized" gap statements online for employees. If yours does not, ask your current advisor to provide a gap statement each year for your employees. E-mail us at info@epsteinfinancial.com and ask for an example of a gap statement.

3. There are a variety of educational materials created by leading authors in the 401(k) industry. We have found the 9 Paycheck for Life Principles from the book, *Paychecks for Life: How to turn your 401(k) into a Paycheck Manufacturing Company*, to be an engaging teaching process that motivates and activates employees in increasing their saving rates and taking responsibility for their 401(k) investment choices. Armed with this information, employees tend to reach out for further guidance and advice.

ACTION STEPS CONTINUED

4. One-on-one educational meetings with employees are the best way to provide customized assistance and create successful retirement outcomes. Be sure to make company time for your 401(k) advisor to provide this valuable service.

5. There are numerous retirement planning calculators offered by your 401(k) record keeper online. We have found the Desirement Mortgage® calculator to be a simple, powerful tool to motivate and empower employees to save more for their desirement years. Go to www.paychecksforlife.org to try the calculator for yourself.

PART FIVE

MEASURING YOUR EMPLOYEES' SUCCESS

FOUR PILLARS OF RETIREMENT READINESS

I t will be valuable for employers to take the time to meet with their advisor and create an Educational Policy Statement that will focus on specific metrics of success they want to achieve in order to impact their employees' retirement readiness.

There are four pillars to retirement readiness we can track: portfolio allocation, savings rates, years to retirement, and the income replacement ratio. Those pillars can contribute to the participant's retirement goals and chances of achieving that "minimum adequate rate of success" for income replacement.

1. Portfolio Allocation: Here we measure how employees are investing. We are looking at whether they are properly diversified for their age. We would be concerned to see employees who are either investing only in one or two funds or are overweighted in their asset allocation selections. We're going to measure portfolio allocation by specific age groups: 20–30, 30–40, 40–50, 50–60, and 60 through to retirement.

2. Savings Rates: We measure everybody's savings rates by age group. We may find that younger people are saving less than are older people, or vice versa. We may want to roll up our sleeves and do meetings for particular age groups to talk about the power of compound interest and why they'd want to save more while they're younger, as opposed to waiting until they're older.

3. Years to Retirement: Here we focus on measuring how close people are to retirement and whether they have saved enough. We can then design education meetings to encourage those individuals who may need to "catch up" on savings. For example, anyone over age 50 can contribute an additional $6,000 (in 2015), known as the *catch-up provision*.

4. The Income Replacement Ratio: In the fourth pillar of success, we calculate each individual's income replacement ratio, as we have discussed. We then create education sessions that teach employees about specific income replacement ratios and how increasing their contributions by just 1 percent or 2 percent a year (automatic escalation) could easily get them back on track to saving enough money. It's the 10-1-NOW Mantra!

A good record keeper can provide every employer with the data needed to regularly measure each employee's income replacement ratio. The employer, with guidance from their advisor, can then target the percentage of employees who need to get on track to saving adequately each year with additional education.

By evaluating these four pillars of retirement success by age groups, we can then customize educational meetings and target the groups that need the greatest education.

A lot of times, people like to be among their peers. If we have people ages 20 to 30 in a group meeting, and we're talking about compound interest and why saving 1 percent more at age 20 could mean having hundreds of thousands of dollars more at retirement, they start talking to one another: "Did you increase your contribution?" And if they didn't, "Why not?" You start to get that cultural influence of peer-to-peer groups encouraging success.

EDUCATIONAL TOOLS AND TECHNOLOGY

The plan's current record-keeping platform also often provides specific investment and educational tools. Many of the record keepers today offer excellent tools for employees to calculate their personal income replacement ratio and personal retirement gap statements.

These worksite planning tools can be an excellent way to engage "tech savvy" employees to take greater control of their financial future. However, we have found that for the majority of employees, you need to first educate them that these tools exist and how to use them.

Retirement Readiness Report

Plan sponsors should request a report from their advisor on metrics for each of the Four Pillars of Success.

We create a Retirement Readiness Report at the plan level, which will show the plan sponsor how our educational efforts and the automatic courageous plan design features are working to impact employee saving and investing behavior. That report will measure the results in all four categories: portfolio allocation by age group, savings rate by age, years to retirement by age, and income replacement percentage by age.

> If you would like a FREE Copy of a Retirement Readiness Report, or would like us to prepare one specifically for your 401(k) plan, please contact us at info@epsteinfinancial.com and say, "Please provide me a sample Retirement Readiness Report or contact me to create one specifically for our company sponsored 401(k)plan."

THE VALUE OF A QUALIFIED ADVISOR

Why doesn't every advisor out there offer these types of retirement readiness services and solutions? Managing a company's 401(k) plan has become a specialty business. It's no longer a field where a generalist financial advisor or just a friend of the family can provide prudent advice and expertise.

If you're a plan sponsor, then you need an advisor who has the experience, expertise, and capabilities to help you manage your fiduciary responsibilities and help your employees create retirement readiness. Your advisor should have retirement credentials, this can be the AIF® (Accredited Investment Fiduciary) designation and/or the AIFA® (Accredited Investment Fiduciary Analyst) designation, both from fi360 (www.fi360.com). Another strong credential is the C(k)P® designation from TRAU, The Retirement Advisor University (www.trauniversity.com). You can be sure these designees have gone through a rigorous curriculum and maintain annual continuing education requirements. Your advisor should also have at least five to ten years of experience managing retirement plans to help fiduciaries navigate the litigious nature of the 401(k) world that we live in today. They must bring a unique process and a success formula that will help a plan sponsor measure the plan's retirement readiness results.

In addition, employees today are overwhelmed and confused by the amount of information on the Internet and in print. When people are confused, they may end up feeling isolated and helpless, which may lead to financial paralysis.

That's why it is critical to hire a talented advisory firm, one that knows how to educate employees about their income replacement ratio so they have greater clarity about how much money they need to save and accumulate, with the least amount of risk during their working years.

The advisor needs to be willing to take the time to educate employees on how to manage that money to create those Paychecks for Life during their desirement years.

Finally, the advisor needs to assist plan sponsors in meeting their fiduciary obligations and maximizing courageous plan optimization using Auto[5].

SAVE AMERICA SAVE ACTION STEPS

1. Be sure to meet with your 401(k) advisor/consultant each year to create an education policy statement and target specific metrics of success you wish to achieve for your employees' benefit.

2. Your current record keeper or 401(k) advisor can generate a Retirement Readiness Report to assist you in measuring employees' savings and investment activity as well as tracking annual progress towards your overall plan goals.

3. A Retirement Readiness Report will show you the Four Pillars of Retirement Success metrics for your plan. It will uncover how your employees are doing in achieving these success levels. Armed with this data, your advisor and record keeper can design a robust education program that targets those employees in each demographic group that need additional guidance and assistance. Email us at info@epsteinfinancial. com to get your complementary copy today.

4. Don't underestimate the value of a qualified 401(k) advisor. They should have at least five to 10 years of industry experience, have at least the AIF® or C(k)P® designation, and an independent investment due diligence and vendor-benchmarking process to assist you in managing your fiduciary responsibilities.

5. To start positively impacting your employees' retirement success and measuring that success on an ongoing basis, be sure to e-mail us for the free reports offered throughout this book. (See the next page for full details.)

GET STARTED HELPING YOUR EMPLOYEES

We hope you have benefited from the information offered in this book. If you would like to learn more about our company and how to engage our services, you can e-mail us at info@epsteinfinancial.com, with any questions that you may have.

Throughout the book, we have offered a variety of free reports that we can send to you as well. Here is a summary of those reports:

1. The Social Security Calculator Report

2. The 10-1-NOW Mantra Chart

3. The Employee Gap Statement

4. The Retirement Readiness Report

To obtain any of these reports, e-mail info@epsteinfinancial.com and simply tell us which report(s) you would like. We encourage you to go to our website at: www.epsteinfinancial.com to learn more about our firm's significant resources and focused solutions for your 401(k) retirement plan.

To Roth or Not to Roth

If you haven't done so already, you should be offering your employees the Roth option inside your 401(k) plan.

The question everyone always asks is, "What tax bracket will I be in when I reach my desirement years?"

And the answer is (loud drum roll, please): "I don't know, and neither does anyone else." Why not? Because the politicians in both the White House and Congress keep changing, and so do the tax rates.

THE GREAT TAX MYTH

Let me share a long-held tax myth. Most people believe that when they reach their desirement years, they'll be in a lower tax bracket. This may be true and it may not.

My father's accountant, for example, told him throughout his earning years that one day, when he stopped working, he'd magically be in a lower tax bracket. And that's what my father planned for. He was a successful executive of a successful clothing chain, and he made a successful six-figure income while he was working. When he stopped working, he had saved enough money so that his income (and his lifestyle) wouldn't have to change.

In other words, he had enough money to generate a six-figure paycheck for life. (Good financial advisor? Yes!)

But something unexpected happened. My dad started his desirement years in 1993, the same year that President Bill Clinton raised the highest marginal tax rates for six-figure income earners to 39.5 percent. Instead of being in a lower tax bracket, my dad was actually in a higher one. (Bad accountant? No!)

The truth is, it's impossible to know what tax bracket you'll be in when you retire. If your income is low to begin with, it's safe to say that, unless you win the lottery, you'll always be in a low tax bracket. But for mid- and high-income earners, this may not apply.

Luckily, there's a strategy everyone can use inside (and outside) their 401(k) plans to avoid this uncertainty.

ROTH INDIVIDUAL RETIREMENT ACCOUNTS

Congress first introduced the Roth Individual Retirement Account (IRA), named after Senator William Roth of Delaware, under the Tax-Payer Relief Act of 1997; however, Roth IRAs were not available until 1998. When Roth IRAs were first allowed that year, they followed the same contribution schedule as traditional IRAs. That is, workers could contribute the lesser of their taxable compensation up to $2,000 per year. That limit was stepped up to $3,000 per year in 2002, $4,000 in 2005, $5,000 in 2008, and today $5,500 in 2015 for under age 50 and $6,500 if you're age 50 or older.

The big difference between the Roth IRA and a traditional IRA is that contributions for the former are not tax-deductible. In other words, your employees pay taxes today on the dollars they contribute. In return, their contributions is not taxed when they're withdrawn at retirement, which is still allowed to begin at age 59.5.

Further, the funds in Roth IRAs must be vested for at least five years, but they're not required to be withdrawn by age 70.5.

Advantages of the Roth

First, your employees will be happy to know that they pay zero taxes on distributions at retirement. There's no cost basis tracking or other tax information required. They simply withdraw the money and it's 100 percent ready to spend. They can also withdraw the contributions at any time without penalty. However, the dividend earnings, interest, and capital gains will be subject to a 10 percent penalty if they are withdrawn before your employee turns 59.5 years old or if the account hasn't been held for at least five years.

For example, assume one of your workers has contributed $100,000 to his Roth IRA, which has grown to $150,000 at retirement. He can withdraw the $100,000 that he contributed at any time without penalty. However, he'd pay a 10 percent tax penalty on the $50,000 earned through dividends, interest, and capital gains if he takes the money prior to age 59.5 or if the account hasn't been held for at least five years.

Second, withdrawals from a Roth IRA will never bump anyone into a higher tax bracket. For related reasons, Roth contributions may effectively be larger than for a traditional IRA, depending on tax brackets. For example, if that same employee is in a 28 percent tax bracket, a $5,000 maximum contribution in 2010 may be equivalent to a traditional IRA contribution of $6,945, since he must earn $6,945 before tax in order to net $5,000 after tax. Since he cannot contribute $6,945 to a traditional IRA, the effective contributions may be larger for the Roth. So, if your employee thinks he'll earn more in his desirement years than he does today, the Roth IRA is the way to go.

Third, Roth IRA contributors will not be required to make the minimum withdrawals at age 70.5.

Finally, because there are no required distributions, Roth IRA assets can be passed on to heirs. Under current regulations, converting to a Roth IRA can reduce the size of a taxable estate. A conversion could allow for decades of tax-free growth. Also, if a spouse is the Roth IRA's beneficiary, the account can be treated as the spouse's own. He or she could forego withdrawals and pass those assets on to children, which would allow decades of compounding—tax free—to work its magic.

Disadvantages of the Roth

First, a Roth IRA is not available to everyone. If you are single and make less than $116,000 you can contribute the maximum annual contribution of $5,550. Your contribution limit will "phase-out" as your modified adjusted gross income (MAGI) goes from $116,000 to $131,000 annually. Once a single tax earner's MAGI is over $131,000 they can no longer contribute to a Roth IRA. For married couples, filing jointly, they can contribute to a Roth IRA as long as their combined MAGI is less than $183,000. Their contribution limits phase-out between $183,000 to $193,000 of their MAGI. Once the MAGI is greater than $193,000 they can no longer make a Roth IRA contribution.

The second disadvantage is that by holding a Roth IRA, employees will also miss tax savings during their working years and may not be able to lower their taxable income now.

THE ROTH 401(K)

In 2009, Congress passed a new law to allow anyone, regardless of their income, to contribute to a Roth inside their 401(k). This is a great opportunity for many high-income investors to accumulate money, either for themselves or their heirs, that will never be taxed. In addition, the contribution limit for a 401(k) Roth is up to the full $18,000 401(k) limit for 2015. This means regardless of your income, you can contribute up to $18,000 as a post-tax Roth contribution inside your 401(k) plan. If you are over age 50, you can make an additional catch-up contribution of $6,000, for a total annual contribution of $24,000.

So we're back to the original question: "Do I Roth my money—i.e., contribute it after taxes inside my 401(k)—or do I continue to contribute pre-tax?"

There are tons of Roth calculators available that your employees can use to choose a strategy. The problem with all of these calculators is that they ask what tax bracket they'll be in at age 65 and beyond. Who knows? So here is another way to consider the Roth 401(k) option. First, consider the following analogy. Imagine you're a farmer and you're about to plant a bag of seeds in your pasture. If you had a choice, when would you prefer to pay taxes on the seeds?

The Tax Choice

_____ A. At the time they're planted in the ground?

_____ B. At harvest time when the crop is fully grown?

Option A is the way to go—why not pay tax on the little seeds going in the ground rather than on the harvest coming out? And that's the idea behind the Roth 401(k); pay taxes on deposits today and withdraw tax free in retirement.[15]

---

15 To be eligible for tax-free income two conditions must be met. First, it has been at least 5 years since establishing your first Roth IRA and second, you have reached age 59.5. Certain exceptions may apply. Speak with your tax professional for more information.

Just like having a balanced portfolio, the best solution for most employees may be to have a balanced "tax" strategy solution with more options to mitigate taxes when they begin taking money out of their retirement plan to create "paychecks for life."

For Those Younger than 45

For younger employees (those younger than 45), we recommend putting 50 percent of contributions into the Roth 401(k) and 50 percent into the 401(k). The benefits of this strategy are as follows:

- They get at least half the tax deduction (USM) today.

- They get the benefit of no tax on 50 percent of their accounts during their desirement years (also USM).

- If taxes are relatively high at retirement age, they can draw from the Roth account first and then take the minimum distribution (starting at age 70.5) from the 401(k). If taxes are relatively low, they can withdraw from the 401(k) first and save the Roth funds for later. Anyone placing 100 percent of their funds in either the 401(k) or Roth wouldn't have these options.

For Those 45 and Older

For folks aged 45 and older who already have a balance of $50,000 or more in their pre-tax 401(k), they should fully contribute into a Roth (unless the tax deduction is critical for current income tax planning). This will fill up the Roth bucket with money that will never be taxed and provide a more balanced approach. Once there's a 50/50 balance between the two accounts, they should split their contributions to equally fund the Roth and the regular 401(k).

Remember, these are general solutions—everyone's circumstances are different. Financial advisors and tax accountants are always good resources to help determine the right solution for each individual case.

RESOURCES

Retirement Made Simpler.

www.RetirementMadeSimpler.org

Default Investment Alternatives under Participant Directed Individual Account Plans, Final Rule.

Federal Register. 29 CFR, Part 2550.

October 24, 2007.

http://www.dol.gov/ebsa/regs/fedreg/final/07-5147.pdf

Deloitte Consulting LLP. Annual 401(k) Benchmarking Survey, 2010 Edition. http://www.deloitte.com/assets/Dcom UnitedStates/Local%20Assets/Documents/us_consulting_2010 annual401kbenchmarkingsurvey_121510.pdf

Employee Benefits Research Institution (ebri.org). A monthly research report from the EBRI Education and Research Fund. 2010 Employee Benefit Research Institute. ebri.org Issue Brief No. 349. November 2010.

http://www.ebri.org/pdf/briefspdf/EBRI_IB_011-2010_No349_ EBRI_DCIIA.pdf

Plan Sponsor Magazine. Auto Enrollment Boosts Participation, Hurt Contribution Rates. May 2011.

http://www.plansponsor.com/Auto_Enrollment_Boosts_Partici pation_Hurts_Contribution_Rates.aspx

U.S. Department of Labor, Sample Automatic Enrollment and Default Investment Notice
http://www.irs.gov/pub/irs-tege/sample_notice.pdf

Meeting Your Fiduciary Responsibilities.
U.S. Department of Labor. September 2006.
http://www.dol.gov/ebsa/pdf/fiduciaryresponsibility.pdf

The Pension Protection Act Section 601.
http://www.dol.gov/ebsa/pdf/ppa2006.pdf

401(k) Learning Center
http://apps.finra.org/investor_Information/Smart/401k/000100.asp

The Desirement Mortgage® Calculator
www.paychecksforlife.org/desirement-mortgage-calculator.html

The Paychecks for Life Nine Principles
www.paychecksforlife.org/the-9-principles.html

Suggested Reading

Benartzi, Shlomo. *Save More Tomorrow: Practical Behavioral Finance Solutions to Improve 401(k) Plans*. New York: Penguin Group, 2012.

Nybo, Stig, and Liz Alexander. *Transform Tomorrow: Awakening the Super Saver in Pursuit of Retirement Readiness*. Hoboken: John Wiley & Sons, Inc., 2013.

Epstein, Charles D. *Paychecks for Life: How to Turn Your 401(k) into a Paycheck Manufacturing Company*. Holyoke: 401k Coach LLC, 2012.

ABOUT THE AUTHOR

CHARLES D. EPSTEIN has more than 35 years of professional experience in the financial services industry. As the principal of Epstein Financial Group, LLC and Epstein Financial Services, a registered investment advisory firm, he continually provides corporate retirement plan consulting, as well as wealth management and financial planning services, to business owners, professionals, and individual plan participants. He is designated as a Chartered Life Underwriter (CLU), Chartered Financial Consultant (ChFC) and Accredited Investment Fiduciary (AIF), and is a Qualifying Million-Dollar Round Table (MDRT) and Top of the Table Member. Additionally, Charlie is a Certified Family Business Specialist, from the American College and founder of the Family Business Center at the University of Massachusetts, Amherst.

In 2002, Charlie established The 401k Coach® Program, which offers training to develop skills, systems, and processes necessary to excel in the 401(k) industry. The unique learning environment of The 401k Coach Program provides retirement professionals the opportunity to network, exchange ideas, and learn to efficiently manage their responsibilities in this ever-changing industry. The Coach Program has been sponsored nationally by major financial institutions, such as Nationwide, ING, Mass Mutual, Lincoln Financial and Mutual of Omaha, as well as more than 30 mutual fund companies. More than 3,500 financial professionals have participated in 401(k) Coach Programs across the country.

In 2010, Charlie was elected to the newly created Legg Mason Retirement Advisory Council, comprising 14 retirement industry leaders in the country. The Advisory Council examines the major challenges facing retirement products, service providers, and best practices observed by the industry.

401kWire has named Charlie one of the Top 100 Most Influential People in the Retirement Industry and one of the Top 300 Most Influential Retirement Plan Advisors in the U.S.

An entertaining and influential speaker, Charlie has spoken on many main industry conference platforms, including MDRT, DCPI, ASPPA and CFDD. He has contributed many articles for industry publications, including the *ASPPA Journal*, *Financial Advisor Magazine*, *BenefitsPro*, *Advisors4Advisors*, *RPMI Weekly*, and *NAPA Net*.

Charlie's first book, *Paychecks for Life: How to Turn Your 401(k) into a Paycheck Manufacturing Company*, released in January 2012, has sold more than 14,000 copies thus far. Paychecks for Life and its nine principles are solely focused on teaching Americans to maximize the 401(k) mechanism to adequately save for retirement with a practical and systematic approach without getting lost in technical jargon. Hundreds of advisors nationwide use Paychecks for Life principles to instill retirement readiness for millions of 401(k) participants.

Charlie's multi-dimensional business practices and considerable experience give him a unique perspective on the challenges that face the retirement plan industry; from individual financial advisors to the financial institutions manufacturing retirement products, as well as the many challenges facing plan sponsors and participants in achieving successful retirement outcomes.

Charlie Epstein, The 401k Coach, is available to lead an engaging Paycheck for Life presentation for your company employees and even your employers association. To have him teach his 9 "Paychecks for Life Principles" for your employees or organization please contact us at info@epsteinfinancial.com today.

EPSTEIN FINANCIAL SERVICES

TF: (413) 539-2370

info@epsteinfinancial.com

www.epsteinfinancial.com

INDEX

SYMBOLS

Z

Printed in the USA
CPSIA information can be obtained
at www.ICGtesting.com
JSHW011511260624
65440JS00017B/686

9 781599 325460